Pagan Fleshworks

Cross implant in chest and captive bead ring in hand.

Pagan Fleshworks

The Alchemy of Body Modification

MAUREEN MERCURY

PHOTOGRAPHS BY STEVE HAWORTH

Park Street Press
Rochester, Vermont

Park Street Press
One Park Street
Rochester, Vermont 05767
www.InnerTraditions.com

Park Street Press is a division of Inner Traditions International

LIBRARY OF CONGRESS CATALOGING-IN-PUBLICATION DATA

Mercury, Maureen.
Pagan fleshworks : the alchemy of body modification / Maureen Mercury; photographs by Steve Haworth.
p. cm.
Includes bibliographical references.
ISBN 0-89281-809-3 (alk.)
1. Body marking. 2. Tattooing. 3. Body piercing. 4. Body, Human— Psychological aspects. 5. Body, Human—Symbolic aspects. I. Title.

GN419.15 .M47 2000
391.6'5—dc21
00-035700

Printed and bound in Hong Kong

10   9   8   7   6   5   4   3   2   1

Photographs on pages 18, 49, 89, 90, and 97 by Jeaneen Lund
Photographs on pages 40 and 43 by Maureen Mercury
Photograph on page 94 courtesy of Kathleen Loughery

Text design and layout by Virginia L. Scott-Bowman
This book was typeset in Stone Sans with Metropolis, Myriad Tilt, and Sinister as display typefaces

For Oren—tattooed on my soul

Jeweled chest
implant.

Contents

Beaded arm.

Introduction

I had always wanted a tattoo. Maybe, to a child's eye, the colors were intriguing. Maybe the faded pictures in ink seemed like a cryptic language that only the wearer could understand. At age nine I wrote a poem about tattoos. I was always noticing body art. My parents thought it was an extreme and deviant behavior, if not a permanently ugly thing to do to your body. In my youth, I didn't get a marking.

Six years ago I was beginning my master's thesis on a depth psychological view of modern male tattooing and felt it would be ingenuine to interview and analyze tattooed men without having experienced tattooing myself. Tattoo studios were accessible, and the art was thriving. So I got a tattoo, although it was neither the image I had envisioned in childhood nor in the place I had always thought it would be.

As I examined the marking I chose and its placement, I became aware of the underlying psychological forces that influenced my final choice. From that internal search I discovered an important phenomenon being played out in the world of body modification: that the tattoos, piercings, brandings, and implants that we see on others or wear ourselves are evidence of our soul's need for expression.

The soul is a difficult concept to define. Because of my training in depth psychology, I understand the soul through its imagistic and behavioral manifestations—through the way images resonate with me and produce deep affect. I see my likes and dislikes, behaviors of approach and avoidance, and decisions and choices as reflections of the process of soul-making and growth. The soul gives personal experiences their meaning, just as soul absence or loss is felt in depression or despair. The soul translates particular experiences into our sense of the religious or our encounters with the divine.

By using a depth psychological lens, we can deepen and expand our awareness of the connection between our soul's desires and our outwardly lived life. Depth psychology views all phenomena as manifestations of the unconscious levels of the psyche. It advocates that soul-making or soul expression is the primary activity of psychic life. Since psychic life is governed by the soul's unconscious forces, this form of psychologizing serves to bridge our ego consciousness and our soul-driven unconscious acts.

To aid our work in contextualizing contemporary American body modifications, we will examine various stages of alchemy, tools of active imagination, mythological imagery, and personal stories to identify the herms or signposts of the soul's journey toward fulfilling its highest expression. The soul speaks in the language of metaphor, patterns, and symbols filtering to consciousness through images, concepts, and situations. These images, concepts, and situations, which originate in the metaphorical and symbolic language of the soul, are called archetypes or archetypal situations.

I am an archetypal activist on behalf of the soul. I view the contemporary trend of body modification as evidence of the soul's need for self-reflection and growth, with the body being used as the soul's vehicle for its transformational processes. In tattooing, piercing, implanting, and branding the body, one attempts, through images and symbols worked on the flesh and under the flesh, to hear the voice of the soul as it struggles for growth.

This work is titled *Pagan Fleshworks* because in examining these various fleshworks it honors the diverse or polytheistic expressions inherent in each soul or psyche. I use *pagan* in this work to refer to a broad vision or perspective as opposed to ritualistic religious practices. Originally the Latin word *paganus* was used to refer to the people of the place who were civilians, as opposed to the invading armies composed of Christians or Mithraics that were called alieni. Pagan people kept their local customs and rituals and did not adopt the alien beliefs of their invaders. Thus, "paganism, in the ancient world can be defined as the religion of a localized homeland, which therefore accounts for the great diversity among pagan cults, customs and myths."[1]

My pagan view of the cosmos has no unified, monotheistic, overriding religious structure that can govern or define, universally, how the soul, particular to each of us, should speak. Thus I use the term *pagan* as a polytheistic style of imagining the world. It means looking at the psyche in a "style that welcomes myth, personification, fantasy, complexity, and especially humor, rather than a singleness of meaning that leads to dogma."[2]

In a polytheistic or pagan cosmos, ritual, ancestors, invisible beings and forces, personal power animals, and private divinities define the moral and ethical codes. In choosing to harness these forces through the ritual of body modification, people are separating themselves from a monotheistic worldview that advocates specific and defined routes to accessing a felt sense of the divine.

We live in a desacralized society today. Many have turned away from established religions and instead are trying to revive ancient rituals that were shed long ago, in an attempt to reconnect with the sacred. Life in a desacralized society demands drastic measures to restore us to the balance of our place in the cosmos in relation to the divine. Body modification is, for some, an attempt to create one's own rituals and symbols of meaning to achieve this balance, to create this felt sense of the divine within. Tattooing, piercing, implanting, and branding are sensate experiences (to varying degrees) whose optimal value can be psychic transformation by conscious recognition of the soul's encounter with the divine or numinous through image actualization and the sensation of the marking. Unfortunately, few achieve true psychic growth or consciously reach this goal.

The use of the human body as a vehicle of psychic transformation is not new. It is an old pattern of civilization: an archetypal situation effected in a ritual fashion. Acts of fleshworks date back to some of the earliest peoples on the planet, the Neolithic hunters. And yet the popularization of body modification in so many different strata of our modern society has raised the question, "What is it about our culture that has caused body modification to become so endemic at this time?" *Pagan Fleshworks* provides some important answers to this question. It also looks at why so many are destined to repeat the modification and what steps can be taken to optimize the experience in order for the soul's voice to be heard.

Nose and ear piercings.

1 The Pagan Path

Y ou want a tattoo. You don't know why, but you've always liked the way they look. You don't even know exactly what image you want, or where you'll get one. But you know if you see the right image, you'll do it. Your daughter wants her tongue pierced. She's going to find a studio that will pierce her even though she's under eighteen. A guy you know at the gym has a tribal armband tattooed around his right bicep. It looks great. The checker at the market has five earrings in her left ear, three in the right, and a small diamond under her lower lip, a librette piercing. You wonder, did it hurt? You notice that many around you seem to have some marking or piercing. You wonder why.

An answer to these musings is simultaneously simple and complex. This is not a return to primitive tribal behavior. We are not those people. We are too diverse a population and geographically isolated to belong to a tribe, and very few Westerners would consider themselves "primitive." So if we are not primitive and tribal, what are we?

We are modern people desperate to hear the voice of our soul or psyche, which needs expression. We are desperate to find our own inner images of resonance that tell us who we are. We are searching, through our bodies, for the sounds and images of our own personal gods that have all but gone silent.

Understanding that there are many inner voices and images of the divine within the psyche means that we are returning to a pagan way of seeing the world. A pagan perspective allows that there is no universally prescribed way for humans to come into contact with the divine, nor is there a fixed image of how the numinous looks or feels. Through a pagan vision, the soul or psyche has many faces and voices that need expression.

When we recognize and accept the multiplicity of our own internal images, when we become aware of the myriad life events that both charge and restore the soul, when we accept our healthy need to separate from the status quo, expressing our own individuality and accepting that of others, we are acknowledging the polytheistic or pagan nature of the psyche. Inherent in the explosion of the body arts of tattooing, piercing, implanting, and branding is the honoring of such vision.

There was a time, in our collective history, when everyone had this way of seeing the world: this pagan vision. It was reflected, by ancient people, in their worship of a multitude of gods and goddesses particular to place. These gods and goddesses were not perfect, incorruptible divinities. Although they shared immortality, each had human attributes or flaws that characterized their personalities. For instance, Hera, the sister and wife of Zeus, is remembered for her jealousy and vanity. She never forgave the Trojan Paris for his choice of Aphrodite over her, and Hera would not be satisfied until all of Troy was destroyed. Artemis, the virgin-huntress goddess, could bless those who honored her with abundant hunting while dispensing sudden death with her arrows to those who displeased her. Hermes, or the Roman Mercury, served as a messenger of the gods and a guide for souls to the underworld. Yet as an infant, his theft of a herd of Apollo's heifers revealed his trickster nature, and Zeus appointed him the god of thieves, in addition to his other duties.

What is important to remember about the pantheon honored by the Greeks and Romans is that in their imperfection, they served as reflected aspects of the complexity of human nature. Regardless of the myths that some gods and goddesses practiced infidelity, some threw tantrums destroying cities, while others exercised great wisdom in conferring judgments, all were understood as divine. In the polytheistic world of ancient times, just as the divinities reflected the sparky multifaceted psyche of man, they mirrored back to mortals shards of the divine.

The practice of community ritual was the key to nurturing the connection between the divinities and their worshippers. Feast days, fasting days, pilgrimages to sacred wooded glens, grottos, caves, and temples, brought people together in common purpose. In ritual coming together, they reenacted and celebrated the myths central to their beliefs. Yearly, new members of the community, and those who had come of age, were initiated into the traditions and mystery cults of the city. The polytheistic world was rich with meaningful ritual practices that served to keep the links between mortals and immortals animated.

For ancient people, rituals reinforced the sacredness of earthly life. They understood, as many of us do today, that engagement in the "ritual" of initiation, worship, performance, or prayer required concrete actions. These ritualized actions held more than they literally appeared to contain. A modern perspective on these practices is that "ritual offers a primary mode of psychologizing, of deliteralizing events and seeing through them as we 'perform' them. As we go into a ritual, the soul of our actions 'comes out'; or to ritualize a literal action, we 'put soul into it.' . . . Ritual brings together action and idea into an enactment."[3]

The ritual enactments of ancient people encompassed the deliteralizing of the tasks of daily life, seasonal changes, and developmental stages of aging. Deliteralizing is taking a mundane event or task and honoring it with intense scrutiny. One can take a walk quickly, not noticing the trees that surround the path or the pebbles and rocks underfoot. A ritual walk involves noticing. Deliberate steps and attention to the detail of the motion of the foot as it falls and the trees that sway in the breeze move a simple walk into the realm of the sacred. Through the deliteralization or sacrafication of ordinary life, ancient people were linked to a larger cosmology of the world of their gods and goddesses.

What we are seeing today is the reanimation of those links through new and original behaviors. We are not returning to the worship of the gods and goddesses of Mount Olympus. Nor are our communities engaging in mass rituals. Instead we are witnessing the resurgence of the use of personal ritual as a means of infusing daily life with a sense of the sacred. Modern Western people are using the body as a vehicle to revive their connections to the larger cosmology. The impetus to create a ritualized landscape in which to connect to the sacred speaks for tattooed, branded, implanted, scarred, and pierced Western bodies.

The drive to engage in ritual as a means of understanding deeper levels of one's psyche is an age-old pattern, a motif of civilization. We call these repetitive patterns of civilization—patterns that are practiced in varying forms throughout the world and have been for generations—archetypal patterns.

⚛ ARCHETYPES ⚛

Archetypes are primary images, patterns, and motifs of the psyche. They are patterns imprinted on the soul. In a swift move, we can go from soul to skin and say that tattoo markings, brandings, and raised forms of subcutaneous implants are archetypal images that have come to consciousness, or have been actualized to consciousness. These images—circles, crosses, angels, skeletons, hearts, she-devils, serpents, fish—derive from a primordial place in the psyche, and when they actualize, when they come to consciousness, it is with intentionality and value. But what is this primordial realm of the psyche? Where in the psyche do these patterns and motifs lie dormant, just waiting for a form in which to actualize to consciousness?

An answer to these questions is found in C. G. Jung's structure of the unconscious. According to Jung, there are four realms of consciousness: ego consciousness, the personal unconscious (or what people typically call "the unconscious"), the collective unconscious, and the psychoid realm. For our purposes, at this point, we will examine the first three.

Ego consciousness is the realm in which we operate in our daily lives. This is the "I" field, our identity, as in "I am." This is the calculating, rational voice that makes decisions. It is the "I" in ordinary reality that drives a car, pays bills, and goes to the market with a shopping list. It is the "I" that remembers where you were the day John F. Kennedy was shot, or how you spent your last birthday. It is the "I" that also walks through the landscape of dreams, interacting with dream figures and images. It is the "I" that remembers those dreams and writes them down.

The ego likes to be in charge of the show in one's life and demonstrates the strength of its authority by repressing what we consider to be "bad" or "wrong" thoughts or behaviors, while allowing "good" or culturally sanctioned "correct" attitudes to form our ego persona. The result of this separation of "good" and "bad" is that the ego becomes disturbed when little nagging internal voices challenge and contradict its "good" decisions. There are very few situations where there are no conflicting inner voices. These inner voices are sometimes portrayed in cartoons as an angel on one shoulder and a devil on the other: both whispering in our ears at the same time. These little nagging repressed voices belong to the field of the unconscious nearest to the ego. Jung called this field, just below ego consciousness, the personal unconscious.

The personal unconscious is just that: uniquely personal. In this realm one

Well-keloided scarification of gravestone rubbing.

relegates thoughts and behaviors that are unacceptable to ego. Feelings of insecurity and rage at your family or coworkers; ideas of what constitutes "wrong" behavior; desires that your parents, church, or state have deemed unhealthy; and cultural taboos are all banished to this realm of consciousness. The contents of the personal unconscious realm were once conscious, once known and understood by the ego, but were then pushed away because they conflicted with the persona, or mask, we wear to function optimally in the world.

An example of the personal unconscious at work might look like this: You want a tattoo, but from the time you were young, your parents have told you that only criminals, gang members, sailors, or whores had tattoos. So when you go to get one, your ego and your personal unconscious have a struggle. Ego wants to have an image put on the inside of the left ankle, but personal unconscious says that you are doing something unacceptable and wrong. The angel on one shoulder and the devil on the other are both whispering.

The end result is that you get the tattoo . . . and have mixed feelings of shame and excitement. You've broken a personal taboo. You've violated a familial and cultural code of "correct" behavior. Yet at the same time, you've activated an important inner structure that demanded an archetypal ritual of initiation, a threshold crossing. You emerge from the studio knowing something in you has changed. Something akin to a private sacred act has happened to you, and you are wearing the badge of that rite of passage. So you wear long pants in public and eagerly roll up the hem to show all of your friends your new tattoo. But you wait to show your parents—even though you are an adult.

Since the personal unconscious is composed of what you, personally, need to repress to function in your life, its contents most probably will be quite different from anyone else's. That is why it is called the personal unconscious.

According to Jung, there is another deeper and more profound field of the unconscious, which he called the collective unconscious.* He postulated that the contents of this realm were the common foundation of our human species. Archetypes are part of this foundational realm. In terms of tattooing, branding, scarification, or implanting, this means that basic shapes and patterns (circles, triangles, lines, spirals, animals) are common and resonate with all humans. Where this gets personal is that these shapes come to consciousness and are then manifest in an

---

*Jung also called the collective unconscious "the objective psyche." For continuity, we will use collective unconscious.

**Archetypal
tattoo.**

image that resonates, or has meaning, specifically for you. For example, a Dinka woman living in the Sudan has a keloided scarification in a chevron pattern on her face as a clan identifying mark,[4] while an American football player has a keloided scarification of the Greek letter omega just below his left bicep as a fraternity identifying mark. These basic patterns arise from the same place in the psyche, the field of the collective unconscious, and are formed and re-formed to provide meaning and value for each individual.

The fact that each image that forms has meaning and value to each of us, in our particularity, brings us to another important aspect of archetypes: their meaning and value is determined by their charge. What is it about a certain image that makes us choose it over millions within our field of vision?

A simplistic scenario to highlight this question is the following: You go to the department store to buy a new pair of shoes. You look at dozens of pairs until suddenly one pair stands out. "Aha", you say, " I want to try on those light brown ones." Maybe the color influences your choice, maybe the style. Whatever the reason, something made you select those particular shoes among many. That choice is an example of resonance; the "aha" is an example of the charge of that resonance.

The charge of an archetypal image registers with our bodies as affect; there is a feeling-tone associated with the charge. We often have a body response. The visceral response can range from mild (as in choosing a pair of light brown shoes) to very intense. Another response to the simple act of choosing shoes in a department store may look like this: You eye the shoes on display and your gaze rests on a pair of light brown loafers. You get a sick feeling in your stomach because a teacher at your elementary school wore shoes similar to those. The teacher humiliated you in front of the class. You leave the store without buying any shoes, as quickly as you can. In this case, a pattern of shame and humiliation has risen to consciousness. It was activated by seeing the shoes, but it was the situation in which you felt humiliated that was archetypal.

We are affected positively or negatively in the presence of archetypal energy. It is the interface of primordial patterns of the psyche and life events and associations that registers as intense affect. Or, we can say that intense affect is felt at the moment of charged archetypal actualization, the moment of conscious awareness of the thought or feeling.

Since archetypes are fundamental psychic patterns and motifs that are fleshed out and actualized to consciousness by specific imagery that is highly personal in its resonance, the charge of that image coming to consciousness can produce either an intensely positive or an intensely negative affect. The intensity of the positive or negative charge is directly related to our earliest associations to the image.

Our reaction, either positive or negative, to the actualizing archetypal structure or image is based on the complex that has developed around the archetype. Complexes are the central organizing elements of the collective unconscious, composed of a shell and its archetypal core. Just as an infant requires adequate oxygen for survival, it requires adequate parenting for psychic health. The primary experiences of parenting are organized by the developing psyche and constitute the beginning of a "mother complex" or a "father complex." The shell is the reaction pattern formed and stored in the personal unconscious; it is activated when archetypal material actualizes.

Looking at the archetype of "mother" provides an example. Everyone has an association to the word *mother,* in whatever language the word is spoken. The word can elicit feelings from mild to extreme. If you perceived your earliest experiences of your own mother as positive, then the archetype "mother" resonates pleasantly with you. If, however, your earliest experiences were those of perceived abuse or abandonment, then the archetype "mother" will cause you to feel distressed and uneasy. That reaction will be projected onto any female who tries to relate to you, even if she does so in a loving way.

The archetype comes to consciousness from the realm of the collective unconscious, but it is the negative contents of the personal unconscious that color how the ego, or you, actually perceive the physical manifestation, either imagistically or energetically.

There is polarity inherent in archetypal imagery that is based on the degree to which a complex is activated or mitigated. For instance, two people in a tattoo studio looking at the same board of flash (tattoo design)—let's say the image of a cross—can have quite different reactions. One person may want to wear that image as a tattoo or implant because his associations to it are quite positive. To him, it may signify the strength of his faith, a righteous way of being in the world, and the philosophy with which he was raised. Another person observing the same symbol may feel anger and disgust based on early negative experiences with religious leaders, or perhaps may feel nothing at all (there is no resonance).

Combining the two elements of image and charge, we now can see that when archetypes of the collective unconscious actualize to consciousness, they carry a charge that is felt in the body as intense affect. Whether or not that affect is perceived as positive or negative directly relates to the repressed feelings and associations that we have relegated to the personal unconscious. In other words, when charged archetypal material filters up to consciousness, it must pass through the sieve of the personal unconscious, where it obtains its form, coloration, and degree of charge. It passes through all of our repressed material. This repressed material has usually only briefly seen the light of day, or been conscious. Hence it is primitive and very often negative. This primitive and negative material is often known to us as the "dark part" of the personality. Jung called this part of the personality the shadow.

⫸⫸ SHADOWBOXING ⫷⫷

Archetypes are experienced in their polarity at various places on a spectrum of "good" at one end and "bad" at the other. This polarity is part of human nature. When only that which we are told is good is allowed to exist in the persona, and when bad is repressed, those elements that we have repressed do not gently fade away and disappear. They remain just below the surface of our ego, waiting to be activated.

One way we can feel their activation is to notice what "triggers" us. When we are "triggered" we often get enraged and say and do things to others that we regret later. "I don't know what came over me," is often said. We have vented something from within ourselves and projected it onto another person. We know our own "dark parts," or shadow, through our projections. The enemy is always "the other" out there.

A liberal Democrat may despise a conservative Republican because unconsciously he fears his constituents may see the conservative side of his own nature. An Evangelical TV minister may preach vehemently against con men yet know he is misappropriating church funds. An obedient, bright child may pick on or tease slower children because she was called stupid by her mother and fears this in herself. The shadow is always lurking just below ego consciousness. It may make itself known to the ego through dreams or, in the case of body modifying, through one's choosing a tattoo, implant, or piercing completely outrageous and incongruous with the persona of daily life. To forever repress the shadow elements of the psyche is impossible. One's shadow will bang on the doors and windows of consciousness and, if left unchecked, unconscious, or ignored, will emerge as compulsions and chaotic drives.

First generation horns and beaded arm.

When the shadow is projected in scapegoating or blame, the goal is to vindicate oneself as a carrier of evil.[5] This is the form the shadow takes as it is projected onto others: the evil is out there. This can easily be seen in "military mentality." The projection of the United States in identifying Saddam Hussein as the leader of an evil empire vindicates the United States from wrongdoing as it bombs Iraq. All wars are predicated on the projection of evil assigned to enemy forces.

Yet it is the mythic form of shadow projection that pertains to the question of why tattooing, piercing, and other forms of body modification are so endemic to our culture at this time in history.[6] In mythic shadow projection, we assign the value of all good and the protector of correct values to a deity or figure outside ourselves, and in doing so, we assign evil elsewhere too. In the West, this projection is assigned to archetypal religious symbols familiar and understood by mass culture.

The dominant culture's traditional Western religious archetypal symbols do not contain polarities: they do not contain the spectrum of positive and negative, good and evil. The Christ symbol is an example of an archetypal symbol carrying only good. Evil is projected onto a different symbol—the symbol of Satan.

The pagan psyche cannot reconcile this split of projected polarities. We all contain light and shadow parts within us. We all react positively or negatively to stimuli in our environment. Where then are the mythic archetypal figures of modern culture to model a balance of good and evil? Where are the mythic archetypal figures of modern culture to show, by example, a healthy integration of the conflicted forces within us? Where do the devil and the angel meet in dialogue and negotiate a balanced position?

Modern times have brought very quickly into Western culture a sense of emergency. Time has been speeded up. The advent of a technology-driven world has activated the archetypal terrain of the collective psyche. For many, especially the younger generation, it is no longer easy to delineate what is good and what is bad. The rules of species survival have changed. As the lines between good and evil are blurred, as boundaries between ethical and unethical behavior are lost, a new order of self-regulation is called forth.

A polytheistic psyche strives to negotiate the tension of opposites it contains. This balance and integration is necessary for optimal psychic health. As the Christ myth loses its grip on the popular imagination, there are no external archetypal figures to carry the projected aspects of good and evil inherent in the psyche. The religious archetypes of Christian mythology, which have dominated the Western imagination for over two thousand years, have lost their charge. An image without a charge is no longer able to carry a projection. When projections don't stick to their projected object, the energy is returned to the sender. The result is that many Westerners are forced to carry the charged energy that they once projected.

What we are witnessing in the explosion of fleshworks is our attempt to find a balanced position in the midst of the hurricane of the changing world order. With no guiding archetypal symbols to contain both light and shadow aspects of the personality, the ego struggles to handle the conflicted charged energy. The result of this struggle is that one may choose to act out (by exhibiting antisocial or culturally inappropriate behavior) or act in (through unconsciously driven body modifications).

Tattooing, branding, piercing, implanting, and other forms of modifying one's body are attempts to contain and integrate previously projected aspects of the individual psyche: all light and all shadow. They are backlash movements in a culture that encourages shadow projection. And, above all, these pagan fleshworks are human attempts to move through the body and find the inner personal divine archetypal structures that unify the soul.

⚛ THE BODY AS LOCUS OF HEALING ⚛

Dave is a thirty-one-year-old male who lives in Los Angeles. All his life, for as long as he can remember, he has had a morbid fascination with death. He says that this fascination became an obsession. He would act out scenes of cheating death by "extreme rollerblading in traffic, darting between cars." He became a pilot. Bungee jumping was thrilling, as he "lived life on the edge." Every night before going to sleep and every morning upon waking he would say to himself over and over again, "I can't believe I'm going to die." That phrase became his mantra, and he'd spend a portion of the day engaging in risky behavior: courting and cheating death.

On a pleasure trip to New Orleans at Carnival, Dave and his girlfriend were walking in the French Quarter when they saw a tattoo studio. He swears that he was not drunk at the time when he made the decision to go in. He had always wanted a tattoo and had planned to get a black panther with green eyes done on his right upper arm. He identified with the panther, feeling it represented his philosophy, "If you cross me, I will attack."

Dave with death tattoo.

When he actually got into the studio, suddenly he found himself discussing another image with the tattooist. As if in a dream, he remembers talking about placing a stylized jazz musician skeleton in a casket on his right upper arm. The refrain, "The life is over but the music lives on" kept running through his head.

He got the tattoo and sensed, as he left the studio, that a huge burden had been lifted from both his body and his soul. He felt light-headed. His breathing was easier, his walk more buoyant. Slowly, in the weeks and months that followed the marking, he realized that he was no longer thinking about death. The fascination was gone. The archetype had lost its charge. His hobbies and interests changed, and his relationship to his parents, always rocky, became more tolerant and loving.

The skeleton had its own animation. It held, for Dave, the power of a living image. He noticed that the skeleton in the casket appeared to be floating on his arm, so he encased the whole image in a tattooed border, to contain the image and harness its energy. Admitting that there are times that he regresses and starts to obsess about death, Dave looks to the image and remembers, "The life is over, but the music lives on."

Dave's experience, as we shall see, is not unique. When anything—an image, a person, a situation—holds our fascination, we are caught in the powerful energy of the archetype it represents. The combination of Dave's identifying a symbol of the central archetype of his complex (bringing the archetype to consciousness) and his experiencing the physical sensations of the marking on his skin helped Dave achieve a profound experience. A shadow fear had been brought to light and integrated into his consciousness when he allowed the image to carry the projection of his obsession. Dave instinctively healed himself through a bodily initiation. That he followed his instincts at all was half the battle. In bypassing his ego's disdain and fear of the image he pushed through the ego's conflict and discomfort with his soul's need for the skeleton. Whether or not this marking constitutes a permanent healing of his complex remains to be seen. At least for now, the archetype has lost its charge and the drive to cheat death is mitigated.

Healed hand implants, fresh sternum implants.

2 One House Divided: Healing the Mind/Body Split

No explanation of the rise and proliferation of modern flesh-works would be sufficient without an exploration of the roots of the mind/body split in Western consciousness.

Contemporary life has us spending many of our waking hours seated in a car, seated in a classroom, seated and watching television, seated and working on a computer, and seated enjoying movies, sports, and other forms of entertainment. All these activities do require concentration and mental acuity. Some of them even require developed motor skills. But none engages the entire body in an integrated fashion. None offers any connection to the natural nonmechanistic sensory world. It is not surprising then that we hear the silent scream of the neglected and starving sensate body.

The pagan psyche is longing to integrate thinking functions with the physical, sensate body. This is difficult in modern times because the physical body is increasingly becoming displaced, or dissociated. The essence of a pagan psyche is rooted in place. We see ourselves in relation to others. We contextualize ourselves through our lineage, our ancestors, and our bloodlines. We need to feel part of larger social entities: families, communities, nations. The advent of cyberspace has created a rootless, placeless society, accessed by the seated and thinking. One's place is nowhere or anywhere. We communicate through an e-mail address and locate ourselves on personal home pages. The physical body never interacts with anyone.

A result of this statelessness is psychic and physical numbness. Tattooing, piercing, implanting, and branding are means of jump-starting sensate functioning that has lost its capacity for feeling.

CRIMES AGAINST NATURE

A short visit to the seventeenth century will help us understand why so much of our daily lives is spent in a seated and thinking position, how we became so split-off from our natural body rhythms, and how we became so alienated from the natural world. The seventeenth century was a turbulent time in history. We have a healthy distance now, but the people of that age had the foundations of their beliefs swept out from under them. This was the time of Italian astronomer, mathematician, and scientist Galileo Galilei (1564–1642), whose work in 1609 of constructing the first astronomical telescope confirmed the Copernican theory that Earth revolved around the Sun. In using the telescope Galileo saw that Earth was one planet among many in the solar system, and that the Sun was only a star among many stars. Here was irrefutable proof that Earth was not the center of the solar system.

This visual confirmation of the Copernican theory* had a destabilizing effect on people of the times. With this discovery of the infinity of deep space, people began to feel, acutely, their smallness and irrelevance in relation to the vast universe.

Galileo also contributed many theories on laws of motion that were foundational for our present understanding of terrestrial dynamics. These theories began the demystification of the natural world.

With Galileo's new, expanded vision of the universe, the laws of the cosmos were being dismantled and new scientific theories based on mathematical principles

*Nicholaus Copernicus (1473–1543) was a Polish astronomer who first postulated that the Sun was the center of the solar system, not Earth, in a work he completed in a 1530 and published in 1543.

Neck and ear piercings.

were replacing them. Sir Isaac Newton's discovery of the laws of gravity and motion unlocked the secrets of the basic structure of the universe.*

While the mathematicians were deconstructing the natural world, the philosophers were interpreting and reconstructing a philosophy based on the new understandings around them. The English philosopher Francis Bacon (1561–1626) wrote that knowledge was power. He believed that God created man to dominate nature and is reputed to have said, "Our task is to put Nature on the rack and torture from her her secrets." As one of the fathers of the scientific method, Bacon combined observation and repeated experimentation to yield empirical results that could then become scientific principles. He advocated that through science, man could elevate himself from the primitive ancient world, and he labeled false the notion that history was cyclic. To him history was linear, always moving toward progress.

In 1637 French philosopher, mathematician, and scientist René Descartes (1596–1650) was formulating a philosophical position vis-à-vis the world around him that would have consequences far greater than he could have ever dreamed. He published the work *Discourse on Method,* in which he attempted to apply mathematical methods to philosophy. In the study of physical science, he rejected traditional methods of experimentation and relied on rationalization, logic, and mathematics.

Descartes is best known for his work *Meditationes de prima philosophia* (published in 1641), in which he wrote the statement, "Cogito, ergo sum"; I think, therefore I am." This statement declared the primacy of ego perception, placing the ego at the center of the universe, thus launching us into the scientific morass in which we find ourselves today.

The confirmation of a heliocentric solar system and a look at the vast expanse of outer space caused people to feel trivialized by the new scientific discoveries around them. They needed to hear that they still had control over something: that as rational men, they had supremacy in this earthly realm. What the *cogito* in Descartes's statement means is that only that which can be rationally understood, or understood by mathematics, is real. All is open to question and requires mathematical proof of its reality: including the workings of the natural world and the role of God in it. Ego perception rules.

With the adoption of this philosophy, gone was the pagan vision of the world

---

*Sir Isaac Newton (1642–1727) was an English physicist, mathematician, and philosopher. His work with light particles and the invention of a reflecting telescope were in addition to his discovery of the laws of gravity and motion.

with its multilayered meanings based on what Descartes considered unreal, unreliable, and unprovable perceptive tools of fantasy, intuition, and imagination.

Here is the mind/body split at its source. Ego (mind) is on one side and is understood as a total thinking system, including consciousness and subjective experience. The rest of the world—which constitutes the entire physical universe, including plants, animals, stones, stars, and the physical body!—is on the other side, separate from the ego. In the Cartesian vision, the entire physical universe is seen as inanimate, mechanistic, devoid of autonomous feelings, and, as such, is essentially composed of constructs operating on autopilot.

"Hence, on one side of Descartes's dualism, soul is understood as mind, and human awareness as distinctly that of the thinker. The senses are prone to flux and error, the imagination prey to fantastic distortion, the emotions irrelevant for certain rational comprehension. On the other side of this dualism, and in contrast to the mind, all objects of the external world lack subjective awareness, purpose, or spirit."[7]

Look at your daily activities. How many of them keep you split-off from the natural world? How many jobs allow intuitive hunches and imaginative, unproven solutions to problems? How many jobs have you sitting and thinking? There is a premium, in our culture, assigned to those who can live within this paradigm. Schools are designed for seated thinkers. High paying jobs are designed for seated thinkers. But we are embodied souls, with a core need for integration of mind and body. And as we have seen, what is repressed, what is pushed away in the psyche, will reassert itself and shout until it is heard.

The adoption of the Cartesian philosophy " I think, therefore I am" has led us to the place of technological advancement in which we live today. The cost of that statement has been enormous. In the devaluation of animals and nature we are witnessing the advent of apocalypse. The devastation of global ecosystems and the extinction of many animal species are easily observable phenomena. What is not so easy to observe, at first glance, is the damage an egocentric philosophy has done to those of us in the West who live under the Cartesian paradigm. This paradigm has split us off from nature, and from the honoring of imagination, and by extension, has split us off from the sacred matrix of connection to the cosmos. And we are paying with our souls.

The pain of this separation from the sacred web is driving many back to the physical body for healing. It is an instinctive, intuitive movement. A movement designed to reanimate forgotten and deadened areas of the psyche through a somatic, or body-felt, experience.

⋙ THE INITIATED BODY ⋘

Tattooing, piercing, branding, and implanting the body are, at a basic level, rites of initiation that attempt to heal the mind/body split. They integrate the impulse to get a modification (whether conceived consciously or unconsciously) into a living body part through the ensuing sensation of the marking.

Initiatory experiences are threshold phenomena that move the intent of the ego from a former state of being to a larger, more expansive state. When one engages in a threshold crossing, the gates between our levels of consciousness—ego, personal unconscious, and collective unconscious—swing open, if only for a moment. An initiation through body modification creates a sensate threshold crossing, testing one's endurance for pain, while leaving the initiate with a badge of the crossing. This form of initiation gives physical witness to significant life passages—a permanent marking or manifestation of a life-altering experience or transition.

The human need for significant threshold crossings is an archetypal desire. We long for a measure of our strength, courage, or endurance—it is inherent in our souls. In ancient times the movement from adolescence to manhood was accompanied by elaborate rituals to mark this most dramatic transition in a man's life.* The rituals were designed to ensure the initiate's full participation and cognizance of the significance of the passage. Initiation into the society of men marked the irreversible direction that a man would take as he assumed his role within his tribe.

The capacity of a body modification initiation to produce a psychologically transformative experience is based on the level of consciousness with which the participant enters the process. The greater the level of consciousness, the greater the psychological transformation. "Without some level of ego participation either through enactment and/or self-reflection, ritual becomes ritualism."[8]

The ritual of a threshold crossing is vital to our personal growth and is often sought at times of life transition. It is only through such transition rituals that we become who we are meant to be. This life process, this personal becoming, Jung termed *individuation.* Often this drive, which originates in the realm of the collective unconscious, has little to do with what your ego thinks you will become. Jung

---

*In Aboriginal society, handing over the adolescent boy to the older men symbolizes the introduction of pain, death, and responsibility into the joyfully carefree and erotic woman-based security of childhood.

Two hands
implanted.

Nose piercing.

believed that this urge was so strong that it forced shadow material to consciousness and had the power to shape one's destiny.

According to Arnold van Gennep in *The Rites of Passage,* rites of passage can be subdivided into rites of separation (such as funerals), transition rites (initiation, pregnancy, or engagement), and rites of incorporation (marriage). It is the transition rites of initiation that particularly pertain to body marking and modification.[9] In indigenous cultures, a transitional rite of passage is marked by three distinct psychic states: separation, liminality, and reaggregation.

In the separation stage of initiatory rituals of tribal cultures, adolescent boys are physically abducted from their villages and taken to sacred places away from that which is familiar. The point of the mock abduction is to separate them from the world of women (the world of their youthful innocence) and return them as men.

Often the boys are blindfolded, wrapped in blankets, or obstructed from seeing where they are being taken. The men who abduct them are masked or painted—in some way disguised. The abduction is accompanied by great noise or commotion. Although all in the tribe understand what is happening, the women of the tribe grieve, and the mothers of the youths mourn the loss of their sons as if they were dead (because, in essence, the youths who have been abducted for initiation will have undergone a death of their innocence and will not return as they were). The physical separation inspires the psychic separation and leads to a psychic transformation.

In our modern culture, there is no clear ritualized separation from parents, loving friends or partners, and the rest of the community when one is ready to cross the threshold into adulthood. In our culture, those ready to make the transition must create their own acts of separation and initiation—often performing these acts alone with no support structure. Tattoos, piercings, and other forms of fleshworks have become a common modern initiation. If the initiate is under the legal age for fleshworks, lying and breaking the law creates an additional separation from the community. The process of getting a tattoo or piercing becomes the goal of the initiation: crossing a threshold of body sensation sometimes perceived as pain. The marking is worn as the proof of that crossing and of the accompanying transition.

By separating from the rest of the community, the initiate moves into a sacred space where linear time is temporarily suspended. This phase is termed liminality, or liminal time. In tribal cultures, this is the time when the myths and mysteries of creation are taught to the neophytes. In liminality, the *sacra* (sacred knowledge) is passed on. Tribal elders and adepts are responsible for the teaching. They are "those who have gone before," or those who have been initiated themselves.

In our modern culture, initiates enter into liminal space at the moment they enter the studio with a tattoo, piercing, branding, implant, or scarification in mind. Sadly, the myths and mysteries of our Western tribe are only revealed to the extent that the artist administering the marking is conscious of the significance of the initiatory process.

In the tattoo or piercing studio, as in traditional tribal rites of passage, the natural world is forgotten as the chosen body part receives the marking. One has the impression that time is temporarily suspended. At this moment, as in tribal cultures, the initiates are mythically linked to the marked ancestors who have preceded them and to those yet unborn who will search for their own form of threshold crossing.

The reemergence from the liminal stage, when suspended time begins again to move in a linear fashion, is called ludic recombination. In an initiation through body modification, this is the closing moment of the ritual, when the wound is complete and bandaged and the novice receives aftercare instructions.

The last phase of a ritual threshold crossing is the reaggregation into the community. At this stage, the neophyte returns to the tribe a changed man, or in contemporary society, the initiate leaves the studio wearing the badge of transition and returns to the profane world with new experiential knowledge.

In the transitional rites of passage of tattooing, piercing, branding, scarification, or implanting, the body has served as the vehicle for a potential psychic transformation. The marked individuals are removed from the common mass of humanity and reincorporated into a group defined by their having crossed a particular threshold. The crossing is not a simple one, even if the decision to become marked has been arrived at with little conscious thought. The choice to engage a sensate threshold, in addition to a psychological one, places those initiates within the ancient tradition of using the body as a vehicle for the search for ecstatic experience.

⚶ AN ECSTATIC QUEST ⚶

Ecstasy is perceived in the psyche as an encounter with the numinous or divine. This encounter is marked by one's sense of the ineffable, the unknowable, or the religious. A construct of purely subjective experience, one's encounter with the

Arm
beading.

numinous, or the divine, makes sacred events that for others may appear profane or irrelevant. For those who choose body modification and the continuum of sensations that accompany the work as their path for an encounter with a sense of the divine, ecstasy is not guaranteed. We can enhance our chances of ecstatic union with the sacred by observing those who have mastered the quest for ecstasy: the shamans.

No group of individuals has so completely mastered techniques of ecstasy as those who practice shamanism. That the study and practice of core shamanism* is being revived today is no accident. After centuries of living with a scientific paradigm and witnessing the eco-soulular destruction wrought by such, a backlash wave of interest in inner symbols of meaning is asserting itself. Discovery of archetypal symbols and patterns of resonance with the soul prompt a desire to understand and explore one's connection to larger archetypal patterns of the world soul. Core shamanism is a path for these explorers.

Shaman is a word from the Tungus people of Siberia that has been adopted by anthropologists to mean many different things: witch doctor, medicine man, sorcerer, wizard, seer, and magician.[10] The word *shaman,* however, does not carry the prejudicial overtones that the preceding words do. Also, not all magicians, medicine men, and so forth, are shamans. In a traditional definition, "A shaman is a man or woman who enters an altered state of consciousness—at will—to contact and utilize an ordinarily hidden reality in order to acquire knowledge, power, and to help other persons. The shaman has at least one, and usually more, 'spirits' in his personal service."[11]

There was a time, in mythic time, when all of humanity had the gift of direct connection to the divine. One myth of the origins of shamanic connection to the divine cosmos is the following:

> Once upon a time, in illo tempore, in the time of paradise, man and his Gods were able to communicate directly. Gods could smile upon man and bless him with good fortune in harvests, children, and abundance; and man could rant, rave, and humble himself before Divinities when disharmony, pestilence, famine, and death ravished the land. With this dialogue came an understanding

....

*Core shamanism refers to the archetypal practices common to all cultures that practice shamanism. That would include drumming circles, the trance state, the shamanic journey, and accessing the invisible helpers of nonordinary reality.

of the connectedness of Heaven and Earth in the matrix of the divine web. All living things related in mutuality and reciprocity, as befit a divine cosmology.

As the planet became more and more populated, the noises of life and the complexities of living made it harder and harder for man to hear divine speech. He still shouted his issues and bemoaned his fate to the Heavens, but the din of the world began to drown out the divine response. In flashes and glimpses he could catch sight of the numinous; in peeps of birds and squeaks of small creatures and thunder, he could hear the Gods' hoarse voices.

His legs, which in previous generations had allowed him to jump the heights of Heaven, had become heavy, leaden, and earthbound. With his wings clipped and his hearing fading, the heavenly voices grew fainter and fainter until they could no longer be discerned by everyone.

Then there remained only a few, on the vast and bloated planet, who remembered the secret of flight, and how to decipher the speech of the Gods. They were charged with going to the Heavens and returning with healing magic. These people, who could let their earthbound soul shards soar to experience the ecstasy of union with the Divine, were called Shamans.[12]

The journey to divine realms demands that practicing shamans move out of ordinary reality to nonordinary reality, while in an altered state of consciousness. This is not a drug-induced trip. Very particular drumming patterns serve as the springboard for this altered state.* To distinguish states of consciousness, we will use the abbreviations SSC (for the altered consciousness of Shamanic State of Consciousness) and OSC (for the Ordinary State of Consciousness, or how we operate in everyday or ordinary reality).[13]

A prerequisite for understanding a shamanic journey from ordinary to nonordinary realms is the acceptance of a principle basic to indigenous people: there is no difference between what we imagine and what is real. This principle directly contradicts Cartesian thought and challenges our Western scientific assumptions. For those of us raised in the West, the lack of distinction between reality and imagination is a hard concept to swallow. But for indigenous people, what they imagine to happen is as real as what their ego perceives as happening.

The imaginary realm exists as a valid universe in nonordinary reality, and the

---

*Trance music is a staple at raves (large, all-night dance parties), where young people enter into light trance states owing to the repetitive drumming patterns of the music.

ego realm exists as a valid universe in ordinary reality. The two realms are equal and exist as parallel: one visible to the eye, one hidden from plain sight and visible only to the inner eye. Following a pagan vision that there are many facets to the psyche, and that external divinities and internal personal gods reflect those facets, these parallel universes are equally animated. Animals have the ability to convey messages in ordinary reality, although it takes some work to decipher their messages.* In contrast, the nonordinary world, to one in SSC, is animated to the point where animals are plain-speaking guides and helping spirits.

Where practicing shamans and people engaging in modern fleshworks meet at a matrix is their respective desire to experience ecstasy. While shamanic practitioners transcend the body, modern initiates move through the body—marking images, piercing holes, branding designs, and implanting sacred symbols. Intense sensation, or sensation perceived as prolonged pain, is desired by those engaging in fleshworks because at the moment when one surrenders and transcends the pain, there may open a realm of consciousness that Jung called *the psychoid.*

Ego is the outer skin of the onion. As we peel away that skin, the next closest layer is the personal unconscious. Deeper still is the unconscious of world soul with its bubbling and seething archetypal images and charges: the collective unconscious. After peeling away the skins of the onion, we see the core. Now throw the core away and take a deep breath. In the whiff of stinging vapors that bring tears to your eyes is the realm of psychoid archetypes.

As with the vaporous odor of the onion, psychoid archetypes have no form. They are charged but formless. We sense them but cannot see evidence of them in images. Although fundamental core psychic energies, they are unknowable to ego. They are always just on the edge of consciousness—a flash of light seen from the corner of your eye, a deep sense of knowing without proof, an unprovoked cold chill running down your spine.

Because we are talking about primary forms of pure energy, they exist in an undifferentiated form. The typical rules of archetypes do not apply. Psychoid archetypes have no polarity. Pleasure and pain, weak and strong, positive and negative, do not exist at this level of consciousness.

Ecstasy is felt when all of the floodgates of consciousness are open and the charge of psychoid contents is allowed to move freely. Some people liken these

....

*See Dianne Skafte's work *Listening to the Oracle* (New York: HarperSanFrancisco, 1997) for a brilliant account of the capacity of animals to convey oracular knowledge.

Partially
inserted captive
bead ring
implant in
back of hand.

Multiple ear piercings and nose piercing.

moments to touching God. There is no doubt that our physical bodies are infused with numinosum. Just as there is no doubt that our psyches perceive these moments as sacred, in their depth of feeling.

Practicing shamans have the ability to open the floodgates of consciousness at will. They have the ability to connect to energetically charged psychoid archetypes and to feel a body sense of the divine.

Contemporary Western people, for the most part, do not practice core shamanism. It is antithetical to our cultural and religious orientation to even think that we can contact any divine entity outside of a religious institution. Besides, most of us delegate that mission to clergy and take messages from Heaven secondhand. However, those who engage in body rituals of initiation want to make that connection themselves. The connection is the goal of the process. Whether one is conscious or unconscious of that goal, psychoid archetypes are invoked when one transcends the polarity of a pleasure/pain continuum and receives a fleshwork.

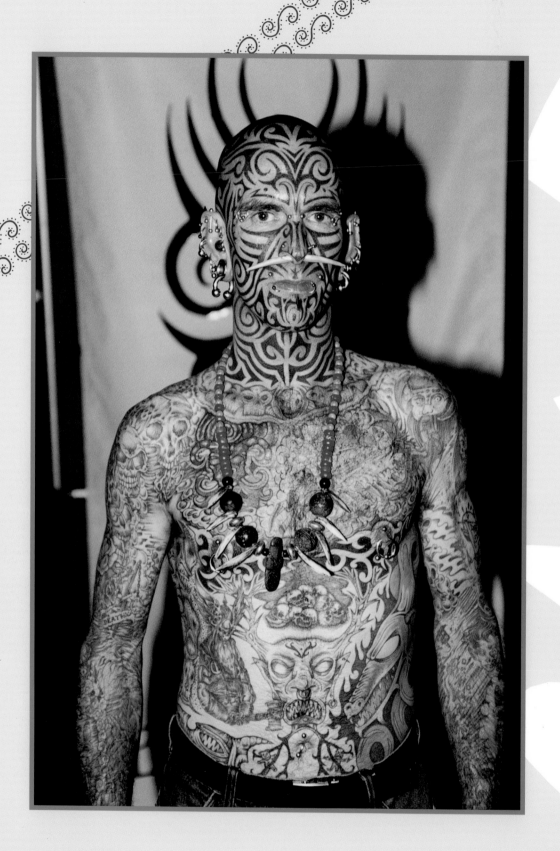

An illustrated man.

3
Psyche as Image Maker

Images of mass culture bombard us every day. We are a visual species: we are susceptible to influence by what we see. Advertisers bank on that susceptibility. Turn on the television. Notice images that refer to place or product. The golden arches, the Nike slash, the Colonel's smiling face, a fat doughboy—all speak symbolic language. Billboards with cowboys riding into the sunset, models with milk mustaches, movie posters, store signs, car decals . . . images abound. These images were created for instant recognition and refer beyond themselves to something larger. That is the nature of images.

⁂ FROM TRIBAL VILLAGE TO SHOPPING MALL ⁂

Images inked on skin are not a new phenomenon by any means. Tattoos have formed a part of archaic cultures for thousands of years. The oldest recorded human to be discovered with markings was found trapped in a glacier in the Italian Alps in 1991. Fifty-three hundred years ago, this Neolithic hunter, whose skin was

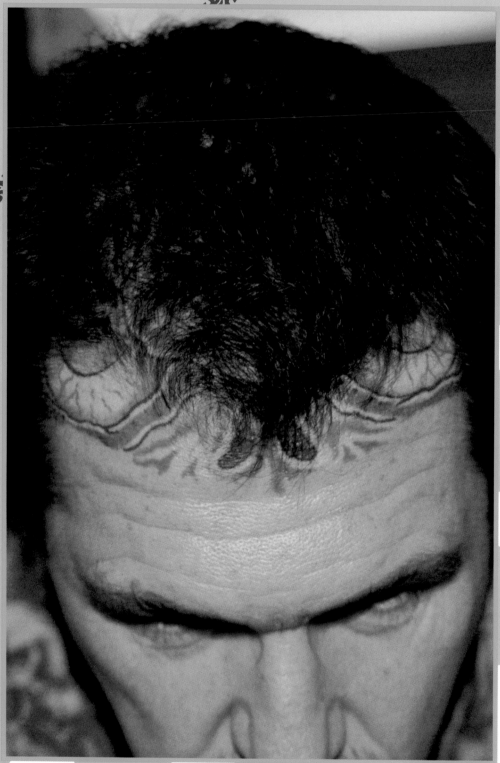

Forehead/scalp tattoo.

preserved in ice, wore tattoos of blue parallel lines at the base of the spine, a cross behind his left knee, and striped lines on his ankle.

Prior to this discovery the first known tattoo was found on the Eleventh Dynasty mummy of Amunet. Amunet was an Egyptian priestess of the goddess Hathor and lived in Thebes around 2000 B.C. Her tattoos were clear and simple: an abstract pattern of dots and lines that included a delicate elliptical design on her lower abdomen, patterns thought to have been fertility related.[14] The same abdominal markings were found on two other female mummies from the same period (one of whom had been a dancer).

In ancient cultures, tattooing was used to assign both positive and negative social status to members of a community. The ruling class, priests, slaves, and criminals were identified by their respective markings. Evidence for this caste system of marking comes from a startling discovery during a 1948 excavation in Pazyryk, Siberia. The twenty-five-hundred-year-old corpse of a nomadic Scythian chieftain, found frozen in a burial mound, was tattooed with elaborate designs covering both arms, one leg, and all across his back and chest. He wore "designs that had been pricked or sewn into his skin with soot to form fish, sheep, rams, and a host of mythical creatures."[15] It was obvious to the anthropologists that the markings were done many years prior to the chief's death, and they were thought to have been badges denoting his ruling position in the tribe. The researchers also noted that some of the markings were intended to be personal, given that they were in places that were covered up by clothing.[16]

The tools and tattoo marking material differ with each ancient culture. Early Egyptians had their designs pricked into the skin with a sharpened bone needle; the tattoo was then made permanent by rubbing a mixture of animal fat and soot into the wound. Celtic tribes tattooed themselves with a mixture of plant materials so foul smelling that those who worked on tattoos were separated from the rest of the tribe. Native American tribes punctured their tattoos into the skin using thorns before mixing berry stains or soot to color the markings. Eskimos created their markings by pulling a soot-covered string under the skin.

Captain Cook is credited with bringing tattoos to Western consciousness. Sailors from his voyages in the late eighteenth century, as well as Cook himself, wrote at length about the natives of Polynesia and their exotic practices of marking the body. It is from these travels that the tradition of sailors getting tattooed derives. The English word *tattoo* comes from the Polynesian *tau tau,* which means to strike. *Tau tau* mimics the sound of a stick being driven by a small hammer into the skin in order to create the marking.[17]

The modern age of tattooing was ushered in with the invention of Samuel O'Reilly's "tautaugraph," an electric tattooing machine, in 1891. Before this time, markings were done entirely by hand, each design laboriously executed prick by prick. The tautaugraph was the prototype for the tattoo machines used today, which execute between "2000 and 3000 pricks per minute, as compared to the 90 to 120 hand-tapped prickings of a Japanese master."[18]

Simultaneously, Lew Albertis (also known as Lew the Jew) changed tattooing forever by his creation of tattoo patterns that could be mass-produced and sold to many shops at once. These templates, now called "flash," sped up the process, so that instead of waiting for an artist to draw out the design of the tattoo, the customer could impulsively choose a predrawn design which could be instantly tattooed.

This is the state of modern tattooing. The clean, accessible tattoo studios with many artists capable of executing flash tattoo designs at the client's whim make it more important today than at any time in history that the decision to tattoo be arrived at consciously. The care one takes in choosing a design will have a profound influence on both the longevity of the image's appeal and the capacity for the soul to speak through that image.

ᙏᙏᙏ PSYCHE'S FACE FROZEN ON SKIN ᙏᙏᙏ

The flash images available for tattoos are not random pictures—they are contemporary images that reflect modern life. They are also images that have endured for centuries and will continue to do so long after the tattooed bodies of today are dead and buried. Pick up any tattoo magazine on the newsstand and see past the gorgeous colors to really notice the images. The most beautifully executed works will be as diverse as the bodies on which they are placed. Traditional designs of 1950s-style hula girls, flowers, hearts, and daggers grace the backs, arms, and legs of many of the models. Tribal art, Native American scenes, Eastern words and symbols, and death imagery can be found on others. Hot rods, eight balls, devils, birds . . . the list is endless. Note the increasing popularity of biomechanical pieces; the images of gears, cables, wires, and robotics augur the new century. It's right there: inked on bodies living today.

The images that a person chooses for marking contain, just in the choice, as much power and significance as the process of getting the marking on skin. The images

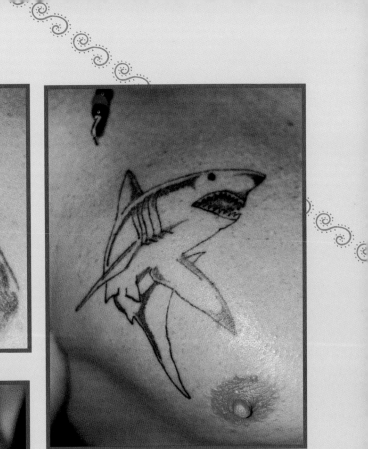

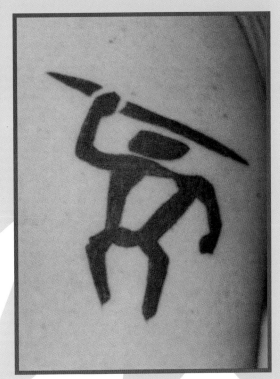

Archetypal images.

Tattooed
leopard
spots.

speak for the neglected and ignored parts of the soul that need voice and are chosen for their resonance and charge. We have discussed that these images arise from the realm of the collective unconscious as primary forms that govern the psyche, or as archetypal images. These are images with qualities of universality: manifesting as psychic motifs or patterns of the soul. They are irreducible primary datum of the soul.

To ask a tattooed person what an image means is bad etiquette. Tattoo images, by nature of having their roots in a deep unconscious realm, cannot be translated into rational concepts and logical explanations. A better approach would be, "Tell me about your tattoo." Then you have opened the door for a peek at the soul. The response may include when the person got the tattoo or the life circumstances that called for a marking, but you will never hear the full story of why the image has resonance. Chances are they don't fully know why themselves. Tattoo images refer beyond themselves to a field of mythic imagination. By isolating an image and considering it for marking, one enters into mythic consciousness, even if one is unaware of it.

If these images come from the deepest part of our unconscious, the question is: How do they then come into our consciousness? They come to consciousness in dreams and daytime reveries, in nightmares, and in fantasy. They also arise when we create art—not for presentation, but just for its own sake. Artistic "doodling" is a wonderful way for archetypal images to emerge from the unconscious to the conscious realm, but too few of us make time in our busy lives for such creation.

In keeping a dream journal—writing down each morning the images, dream figures, and characters that present themselves in dreamtime—one can receive important messages from the soul. By tuning in to these messages you are honoring the unconscious part of your psyche that is speaking and the images it brings forth. Would you not listen politely to a guest in your home? The same is being asked of you here.

Unfortunately in a culture that values rational thinking above all else, there is little place for images from the unconscious in the modern world. These images speak but are, for the most part, dismissed or unheard.

So what happens if images of the collective unconscious are refused access to consciousness? What happens if we ignore or repress the need to honor such images in our life?

Simply put, we become at terrible risk. Failure to acknowledge the power of the mythologems, or archetypal images, that are seeking expression puts one at risk of being inundated by their force. These images form for a purpose: that purpose being to provide information about unconscious processes that ego cannot access. They need to speak and will demand to be heard.

One crosses a threshold by actualizing an image to consciousness and marking it on skin. This may be a sensate, pain/pleasure threshold and/or a psychological one. Moving into the field of charged imagery disturbs ego's boundaries. There may be psychic discomfort in making the decision to tattoo or not to tattoo.

If we do not first seek the images that govern the soul and then honor those images, we will be forever acting out or acting in, in an attempt to mitigate the force of the drives that will result. We will be driven to act upon urges that we will not understand.

It is not necessary to tattoo on the skin all images brought forth from the unconscious realm for optimal mental health! We are not advocating that. But it is necessary to seek out or notice images of resonance and to honor those images as they present themselves.

⨠ TENDING THE LIVING IMAGE ⨠

One way of honoring images (and we would suggest that this be done with images that you would want to tattoo) is to engage them in "active imagination." Active imagination is a technique for amplifying and animating imagery. With the understanding that images do not form and present themselves without intention and do not resonate randomly, active imagination may be used to deepen our understanding of what the image is trying to convey through its appearance. This is not dream interpretation. There are in fact many, many methods and techniques of working with dreams. Some involve association, some offer interpretation, some simply tend the living images as they present. It is not our purpose to explore these methods in this work. We will not analyze the dream at all. Our goal is to choose the most prominent and charged image in this dream and work with it to understand what it is trying to say to the dreamer. This is very deep and psychoactive work. As with any technique that opens a bridge between ego consciousness and unconscious realms, it should be used with care and ideally with the assistance of a professional who is familiar with this technique.

Let's look at the following dream:

"I am walking through a crowded marketplace in a foreign city. It feels like the Middle East. There are many people in the marketplace, dressed in bright clothing and speaking a language I do not understand. I smell spices and dung. There are stalls with colorful cloths, piles of vegetables, nuts and spices, trinkets, and even small animals in cages. I stop at a stall that is selling small animals and peer into a rusted cage sitting on the dirt floor. Inside the cage is a black snake wrapped around a tree branch. As I get closer it suddenly rears back, hisses, and strikes at me. I jump away in alarm and wake up in a panic."

Assuming, for a moment, that this is your dream, we will now animate the primary image with the technique of active imagination. The most charged image for you, the dreamer (and it will always be the dreamer who decides which image carries the charge), is the snake in the cage. Find a quiet place, with minimal visual and auditory stimulation, and have a paper and pencil ready in case you want to write down the dialogue. To engage the image in active imagination requires that you proceed with the understanding that the engagement and dialogue you will have with the dream figure is not imaginary. Remember, we said that indigenous people understood that there are parallel levels of consciousness and that if you imagine something, it has its own reality on another plane, in nonordinary reality. Here you are accessing a plane of nonordinary reality.

Sit quietly (you may want to light a candle or dim the lights), close your eyes, and begin to notice your breathing. It is probably short and rather shallow. Slow it down. Allow your breathing to become deeper and more drawn out, until you feel yourself very relaxed and centered.

Now bring the snake to consciousness. Really look at the snake with your inner eyes. Notice the details that perhaps you did not notice while remembering and writing the dream. The snake's eyes are black. There are grained markings on the skin. A bit of white coils around the tail. The snake is so much longer than the branch around which it is wrapped that most of it is hanging off.

Now it has your attention, and you have its attention. Ask it a question. Perhaps ask, "Snake, why are you in the cage?" Listen with an inner ear and hear the answer. Ask another question, like, "What do you need to say to me?" or "Why are you coming to talk to me now?" Again listen with the same inner attunement. What you will notice in questioning the snake and listening to its answers is that the dialogue will reveal information that at first you may not understand. Ask for clarification. You may even disagree and argue with the snake. Listen carefully and respond with gentle respect. The snake came to tell you something important. Whatever dynamic is played out in the exchange, you have accessed some information that was previously obscured for you.

Finally, close the dialogue by thanking the snake for speaking to you. Dream and fantasy images should be approached with reverence and humility. They came to you for a purpose, and they deserve thanks. Now you may want to read what you have written of the dialogue, or you may want to stay in sacred space awhile to reflect back on the exchange. There is a good possibility that the dialogue has revealed some personal, deep, inner active process or thought about which your ego was unaware.

The last step in an active imagination engagement with an image is to act on behalf of the encounter,[19] or to create your own ritual around what your dialogue has revealed. That may take the form of going to the zoo and looking at snakes, painting a picture of a snake, doing a snake dance, finding a statue of a snake goddess and placing it on your desk, or if you are so moved, tattooing a snake on your body. The point is to engage in a ritual enactment that bridges the realms of the consciousness that have been opened for you to receive this amazing dialogue. The ritual is your choice and it serves to close the realms.

If you decide to actualize that image on your skin as a tattoo, you have accessed through active imagination a profound level of the unconscious and felt the charge of the archetype. Now all that remains is to decide where the image will be placed on your body.

⚡ WOUNDED HEALING ⚡

The placement of a tattoo is not an arbitrary choice. Yes, there are those who say, "I didn't want it to show when I'm at work, so I got it on my shoulder." Or others who will think that the image is private and should only be seen by a lover. But even with these rational, logical maneuvers by one's ego, the choice of left shoulder blade, right inner thigh, inner lip, wrist, or breast has significance.

The body that receives the marking has a need to be healed: the body part has spoken and asked for the marking. The wound may be old, so old that you cannot remember when it occurred. Or you may have had a trauma that you do remember: a near miss at losing a limb, a surgery to repair torn ligaments, a violent body invasion, a heart violation. You have a felt sense that something is needed to quiet the area that is calling for marking, or conversely, to stimulate that area. Tattoo needles puncture the second layer of dermis at about twenty-three hundred insertions per minute. It is like needle intercourse with skin. The sensate response to tattooing is

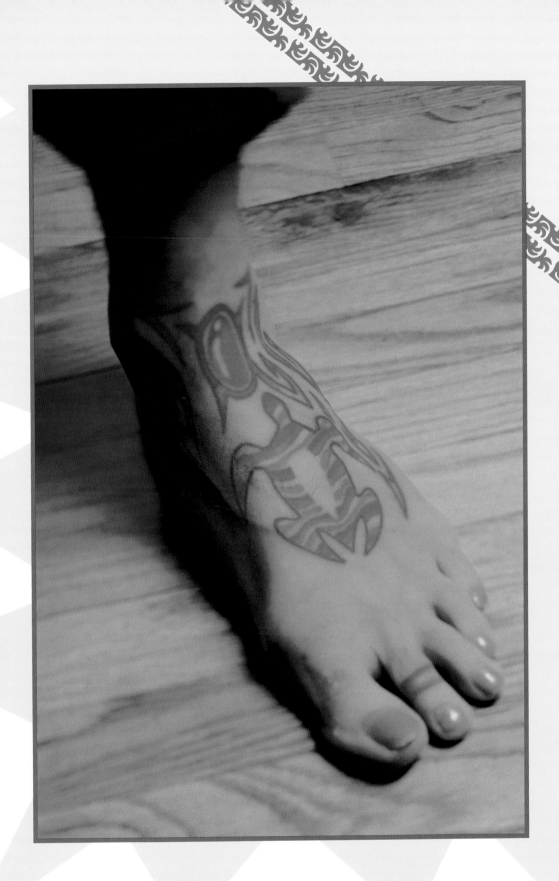

Jeweled
foot.

very subjective. Some people report extreme pleasure: some pain. Most find a sensation somewhere between the two extremes that has them coming back for another tattooing. The marking then becomes a part of your soul history.

The concept of soul being manifest in different parts of the body is not new. Ancient Egyptians removed organs of the dead and placed them in specially sealed jars corresponding to the divinities to which they would go.[20] Indigenous people believed that physical disease was a symptom of soul loss. We chronicle our life journey through our wounds and mark the moments of triumph over them with visible and/or invisible scars.

Karly got her first tattoo when she was sixteen. A runaway from an abusive family, she chose to place a large butterfly in the middle of her back. It was very painful to get that tattoo. She says that leaving home was also very painful, and that the butterfly on her back represents her freedom; it is always pushing her forward.

Jeff got his first tattoo at nineteen. The "God's eye" was placed on his left breast above his heart. He says that he chose the image and placement because he speaks from the heart, and he wanted to protect, in a sacred way, the purity of his heart. The tattooing was painful. The breast area is quite sensitive. But Jeff felt that the pain was necessary to bring the image into his body in a profound way.

A tattoo seen on someone's right wrist inspires the questions: Tell me about the right hand; are you right-handed? Is there something that must be done with your hands that you are reluctant to do? Have these hands done things about which you are ashamed or proud? How do these hands serve you or work against your conscious wishes?

The choice of a right or left side for a marking is not a random or arbitrary one. Based on research of the cerebral hemispheres of the brain,[21] there are split functions performed by each side. The left hand is aligned with the right side of the brain, while the right hand is affiliated with the left. The left side of the brain controls speech and the traditionally extraverted functions of conscious thinking, while the right side makes sense of what the left side sees. The right side of the brain is closer to the unconscious functions of feeling, emotions, and intuition, serving as the springboard for left-brained actions. Thus when individuals decide to tattoo, brand, implant, or pierce a particular side of their body, the answer to the question of what kind of energy they want to access, or what area of their life needs attention or healing, is based on the bicameral brain theory.

These questions may be answered through a sort of "active imagining" of the body part that is speaking for a marking. What is being opened in this imaginary dialogue is the passageway, or corpus callosum, between the two sides of the brain. A depth psychological approach to this information-sharing views it as a dialogue between the ego and the unconscious as images and impulses move from one hemisphere of the brain to the other.

Steve does not yet have a tattoo, but he has in mind an elaborate design of a whale, a shark, and a dolphin forming a circle. He says that he wants it on his right bicep, between the shoulder and the elbow. With a little active imagination work about his arm, he moves the placement up to the shoulder area. That is exactly where he feels the need for a marking on his body. He tells the story of the significance of his right arm, saying that he was a baseball pitcher all his young life and throughout college. He had a chance to go to the minor leagues, but his own pride and stubbornness caused him problems with the coach, which cost him a tryout chance. He still regrets it today, ten years later.

Every tattooed person has a unique story. When we listen to a person chronicle their markings, we hear a soul history unfold.

George wondered aloud about the two tattoos he had on his shaved head. Both were symmetrically placed a few inches just above the ears. He said that he shaved his head so they would show. One was the name of his gang, the other the name of his youngest brother, who had committed a murder at age fifteen and would be in prison for life. When asked to talk about his feelings about the two images, he said he felt very sad about both of them. A few minutes later, he remarked that there were times that he just wanted to "end it all." When saying this, he raised his hands, pointed his index fingers at the tattooed names and pulled imaginary triggers. Suddenly he understood the answer to his own question about the tattoos. "I guess these markings keep me alive. They are my reasons to live. My homeboys are my family, my gang. And my brother depends on me on the outside. I'm all he has. I have to be there for him and my homeboys—for a long time."

Spending time in an active imagination state before marking the image is crucial to the longevity of the image. If one thoughtlessly or unconsciously gets a marking, the image will soon lose its charge. The tattoo removal business is thriving for just this reason. The use of active imagination will allow you to access the deepest resonance of images that seem to appeal. It will connect the image to you and you to it in a relationship for perpetuity.

Spiked head.

4 Portals to Psyche

In the last chapter, we discussed the importance of tattoo images as pictures of meaning. While tattooed images do provide important insights into the issues bubbling in the unconscious realms, and their placement on the body does stimulate affect to the point of effecting transitional life experiences, tattoos remain "skin deep." Piercing, reforming body parts, or implanting sacred jewelry in the body invades the body to a greater extent than tattooing, requiring differently trained artists to effect these modifications.

Tattooing, as a permanent coloration of the second layer of the dermis, does not promote significant blood loss (at most, small traces of blood and lymphatic fluid are lost).[22] Piercing or implanting requires a puncturing of the skin with needles and the insertion of jewelry either through a hole or under the skin. Reforming and restructuring body parts involves the cutting away of excess tissue. All piercing, implants, and reformations draw blood.[23]

Why do people, in our culture, pierce their ears, faces, hands, navels, nipples, or genitals? Why do people reform their ears, or implant transdermal spike holders, jewel casings, or beads that cascade down the shaft of their penises? The answer to these questions is multileveled. On one level this behavior is a simple human need for self-adornment.

Individual self-expression through personal adornment is a drive foundational to the human experience. As we become who we are meant to be, as we move through the process of individuation, we must separate ourselves from others in some way. The soul stretches and grows through separation from the masses. Personal adornment through body modification has the potential to accomplish this goal. Each person is a living canvas of his or her own expression. Bejeweling one's personal skinscape accentuates the uniqueness of each person's soul expression.

Since no two people are exactly identical, no two modifications will appear identical. Thus seven pierced tongues are seven different tongues in seven different mouths on seven different faces. Each of the piercees has had a different sensate response to the piercing; each has gone in with a different reason to be pierced. The adornment factor may hold deep significance for each individual in his or her particularity. For many modified people, this is the only level with which they consciously identify. Although this is a valid reason to seek an implant or piercing, it is the ego that reasons so, and we want to learn from the unconscious what is being played out or activated.

ACTIVATING ANATOMY

We learn about the drives of the unconscious by observing not only the choice of the fleshwork itself but where the piercing, implant, or reformation is placed. As we have seen with tattooing, specific body parts cry out for healing. With this in mind, it is important to understand that as with tattooing, piercing, implanting, or reforming the body is not a wounding or a mutilation of the flesh, it is a homeopathic attempt to heal oneself. We cannot discuss the individual needs of every body part of every person who gets a fleshwork. Each body holds its own history, its own cellular memory or wound. We can, however, look at these fleshworks to see what the psyche has to say.

In ancient times, mythological young gods and heroes depicted as crippled, lame, bleeding, and sometimes castrated were venerated for showing the scars of life's battles.[24] The same applies today. Regardless of the fleshwork, there is a wound to heal. The bearer of such a wound may become a "wounded healer" for others, or that person may simply remain a healer of him- or herself. "Each organ has a potential spark of consciousness, and afflictions release this consciousness, bringing to awareness the organ's archetypal background, which, until wounded, had simply functioned physiologically as part of the conscious nature."[25]

Bear-shaped
implant
in hand.

The insertion of fleshwork needles brings a very particular area of the body to consciousness. Without discounting the enhancement of sexual pleasure attributed to some piercing and implants, it is possible to ask deeper questions of those body parts. Just as we saw with tattoos, these questions may be used as guides for active imagination explorations. The difference here is that it is not the image that is being animated. With piercing, implants, and reformations there is no image to lead the way for one to discern what the soul is trying to say. The emphasis here is on deep listening to the body.

We acknowledge that there are some observations or questions that may or may not apply to specific individuals who have chosen the fleshworks that we will discuss. Yet we offer these questions as guides to an internal dialogue.

Hand-webbing piercing, with barbells between fingers, or implants on the back of the hands, beg the question of what jobs do the hands wish to avoid that they should be so impeded from full functioning. Or, conversely, what have the hands done, autonomously, for which they should be rewarded. Have these hands reached out to others? Has this one hand pushed someone or something away? Are these hands, palms up, giving to the world? Are they, palms down, refusing?

Tongue piercings, immensely popular as first piercings, raise other issues. Besides the possibility of increasing stimulation during oral sex for one's partner, it must be noted that tongue piercings impede, to a certain extent, the speech of the wearer. Inquiry might include: What is it that you are afraid to say? Were you, in your youth, told to be quiet, or to hold your tongue? What part of you is afraid of what would happen if you expressed the inexpressible? How comfortable are you with expressing your strongest feelings of love or rage?

Nipple piercing, on women or men, may either stimulate or deaden the areolae by the formation of scar tissue around the jewelry. Jewelry implanted in the chest area, between the breasts, raises the same questions as nipple piercing. Breasts are associated with nurturing. Whether nurturing oneself or others, the heart lies behind the breast. What part of you needs nurturing now? Is the goal of the piercing to stimulate or numb the nurturing capacity? Are you too giving to others? What is left for you at the end of the day? Have you been wounded by love and are now numb to those feelings?

A clitoral hood piercing may increase stimulation of the clitoris or bring sensation to an area of sexual trauma that has been kept psychically numb. Yet there is always the danger that a clitoral piercing may deaden the sensation of the clitoris as well, by the formation of scar tissue around the jewelry. This piercing asks the

Split
tongue with
piercing.

wearer to access her libido. Where is energy and stimulation lacking in her life? Labial piercing jewelry may celebrate the sexuality of the wearer or demand that the question of why the vaginal opening needs decoration be asked.

Penile piercings or beads implanted on the shaft of the penis serve a primary purpose of enhancing sexual stimulation for the wearer or providing increased pleasure for both participants in intercourse. A ring placed in the position of a Prince Albert piercing (a piercing through the urethra at the base of the penis), as well as barbells pierced in ampallang (a barbell placed horizontally through the head of the penis) or apadrayva (a barbell placed vertically through the penis shaft behind the head), is often done to restimulate nerves of the circumcised head of the penis. One might ask of these fleshworks: Where in your life are you feeling impotent or numb? What kind of power or strength do you need to advance in your life? What areas of your psyche are asking for stimulation?

A subincision, or splitting of the penis, is a reformation modification. This is an ancient practice of indigenous people that has made a dramatic return to modern society.* In tribal societies subincision is done to give the tribesmen the psychic wholeness of both male and female. The splitting creates a female opening for the male, with the blood of the cut mimicking menstruation. The tribesman is then related to the mythic androgyne of original creation who, as the first being on earth, embodied both genders. The traditional reasons for this modification are, for the most part, not in the minds of contemporary men who receive these modifications. Instead many seek this reformation for the resensitizing of the penis with fresh new nerve endings exposed on the penile shaft. But there are always deeper questions that may be asked of those who subincise. For modern men seeking this modification possible inquiries are: Where is your life out of balance? Are you caught in a masculine stereotypical role that needs shattering? Where, in your life, is a place for sensitivity, emotions, feelings, and intuitions (the traditionally "feminine" qualities)? What events have deadened your libido?

The questions we have posed are theoretical. There are many more that may be generated through an active imagination dialogue with the body part that wants a fleshwork. The dialogue is critical because there is a direct connection between the capacity for a fleshwork to heal psychic wounds and the consciousness one brings to the modification process. If that dialogue is ambiguous or

---

*For a more complete description of indigenous subincision rites, see Robert Lawlor, *Voices of the First Day* (Rochester, Vt.: Inner Traditions International, 1991).

unclear, and one still feels a strong desire for a modification, then there may be energetic forces at work in the anatomy that the ego cannot understand.

Needle punctures from piercing, implanting, or reforming one's anatomy create holes in the body. These holes are portals. They are portals for energy to be released, for energy to be taken in, or for trapped or stuck energy to be stimulated to flow again from one place in the body to another. The energy centers in the body that promote this kind of healing are called *chakras.*

⋙ THE CHAKRA CONNECTION ⋘

There are seven chakras in the body's energy field: the root or base chakra, the sacral plexus chakra, the solar plexus chakra, the heart chakra, the throat chakra, the third eye chakra, and the crown chakra. Energy moving through the chakras induces particular psychic states. Since each chakra has its own energy field associated with our emotional body, particular fleshworks may stimulate and activate certain feelings, thoughts, or images that usually remain unconscious.

The root or base chakra is located at the perineum, between the anus and the genitals. This is our lowest body energy center, and it is here that we ground ourselves in life. Genital piercing, bead implanting, or genital reformations are some ways to bring us back into awareness of this chakra. The root chakra is associated with the will to survive: species survival. This is the seat of our most primal drives and of some of our greatest sensate pleasures. Our potential power rests in this chakra. It is from this chakra that energy rises and flows through the body.

The combination of actual stimulation of the root chakra and the power of the psyche to internalize transformational events can be seen in the following story. Rob, in his late twenties, had been trying to impregnate his wife for over a year. He was unhappy at work because of a dominating, unsympathetic boss and fearful of losing his job. His perceived impotency at home and his inability to change his work situation left him feeling depressed. He had been tattooed twice and liked the feeling of the needles on his skin. This time, he decided to do something radical to jump-start his libido. He chose to get a dydoe piercing. This piercing of his penis, done through both sides of the upper edge of the glans, healed slowly.

He felt that from the moment he got the piercing, a change in his life was imminent. As he tended the wound and it healed he noticed an increase in his sexual desire and sexual pleasure. His wife became pregnant. Confident in his ability

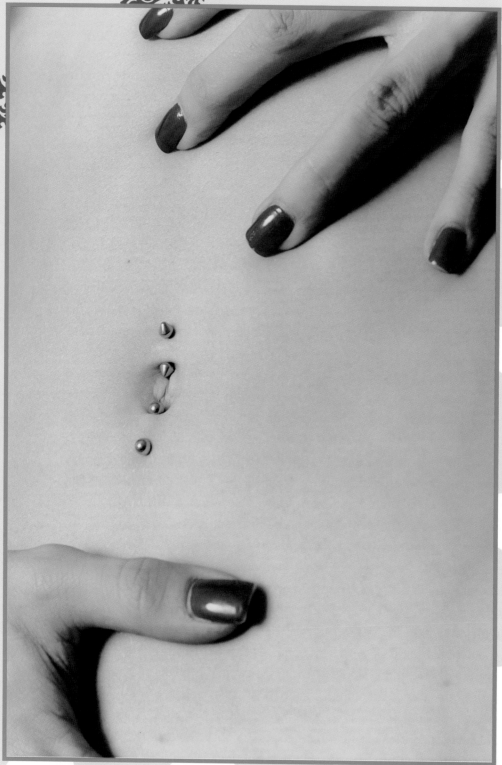

Navel piercings.

to perform at home, he took the risk of finding a different job with less stress. With the root chakra energy awakened from its stuck and blocked position, the balance returned to his life and he was able to function at his optimal energy level.

The next chakra, moving up the body, is the sacral plexus. In women this chakra is the womb and domain of the reproductive organs. Seminal fluids, menstrual fluids, and urine are also associated with the sacral plexus chakra. It is the chakra of base emotions, lust, and sexual vitality. The sacral plexus chakra is closely associated with the base chakra in that it is a primitive realm in which visceral responses to archetypal images and situations are sensed.

The solar plexus is the third chakra, located behind the belly button. As this is the chakra of the abdomen, eating and digestive issues are felt in this chakra. Navel piercing is one way to bring attention and energy to this chakra.

A fortyish woman, overweight most of her life, had her navel pierced as a testimony to her resolve to love her body despite its size. Her issues around dieting and food had dominated her psyche since childhood. The piercing removed that factor and she began to radiate self-confidence and pride in her appearance. The opening portal of the navel piercing allowed stuck and congested energy out as well as allowing in new and vital psychic changes. The third chakra is also the seat of gut feelings and the house for anger. Unexpressed anger may stay in this chakra for many years, blocking the will to individuate. Since the solar plexus chakra is closest to the spot of the umbilical cord, old patterns, emotions, and crippling complexes may be released with modifications at this chakra. Perhaps the popularity of navel piercing has less to do with adornment and more to do with releasing the emotions blocked in this chakra.

The heart chakra is the fourth in the energy chain. This is where the affect of love is felt, as is pain and sadness. Nipple piercing, chest implants of beads, hearts, and crosses, and transdermal jewel casings serve as talismans against pain and sadness. This is a very sensitive area for body modification work because there is little fat as a buffer to the nerve endings under the skin. Compassion and intuition may be opened and expanded by body-modifying work connected to this chakra, while despair and hard-heartedness may be released. The energy stimulated in this chakra has the power to stimulate a change of heart.

The fifth chakra, which is dominated by sound, is the throat chakra. Sounds of pain, pleasure, grief, joy, or song emanate from this energetic realm. The throat chakra may express what the heart chakra has opened. The skin at the throat chakra is thin, making all modification work very painful. Thus when stimulated by some modifications, the fifth chakra may cause a release of powerful sounds giving voice to that which was unexpressed.

Marko, "the Hawk," is an award-winning Ultimate Fighting Champion. When he began his career, he developed his skill in winning minor cage matches but lacked the confidence to fight the semiprofessionals and work his way up to the big league. He got his first tattoo on his lower back, at the spine. This tattoo stimulated the energy of the sacral plexus and his career took a jump. But it wasn't until he tattooed the Chinese name "Lu Tung-pin"* on the right side of his neck that he began to win more difficult matches and advance his career. His unique signature is the sound he makes when fighting. What emanates from his throat is a primitive guttural battle cry as he lunges at his opponent, and a victory yell at his win.

The third eye chakra, located between the eyebrows, is the sixth chakra and it represents energy movement between the ego and the unconscious. The energy of this chakra houses inner sight, inner knowledge, and internal dialogue. It is the chakra of the inner eye that we use for active imagination work. Piercing the bridge of the nose, the nose itself, the septum, eyebrow, and under the lower lip (librette) all follow the line of this chakra. Implants in the forehead or brow area all serve to activate the energy of the third eye. This activation has the capacity to open one creatively and to expand one's vision to allow unconscious material to filter up to ego consciousness. When the third eye chakra is animated, the negative energies of narrow-minded thinking, dominating and controlling behavior, and egocentric willfulness may dissipate.

Lastly is the cap of energy release or reception in the crown chakra, the seventh chakra. The top of the head is quite sensitive to receiving energy or releasing it. Horn implants and spikes implanted in the head stimulate the crown chakra. One feeling alienated from life or depressed would charge this chakra in the hope of releasing the psychic pain. Divine blessings shower the body through this chakra, or energy may be sent upward through the same portal.

There are specific exercises for bringing attention to each individual chakra and for moving energy through the body so that each chakra receives a flow. Before piercing, reforming, or implanting a chakra area, an attempt should be made to work with energy movement and engage the chosen body part in an active imagination dialogue. When the chakra has spoken of its blockage or need, then a more

---

*Lu Tung-pin is a Chinese deity, one of the Eight Immortals of Taoism, revered for his healing abilities, his capacity to slay evil, and his ability to overcome difficulties with his magic sword.

Pierced face.

conscious decision to stimulate the area can be made. This method will optimize the body-modifying experience and will promote deep healing.

We have seen that the drives of the soul may lead one to heal old cellular or psychic wounds, access the energetic healing power of the chakras, and satisfy one's need for unique adornment. Part of the appeal of fleshworks as personal adornments is their ability to call attention to the wearer. Yet as an adornment becomes more prevalent in the culture, it loses its novelty and ability to be note-worthy. For those who seek to create a distinctive look for themselves, it is then necessary to seek out more unusual and extreme modifications for self-expression. One person who is devoted to pushing the art of body modification to new limits and standards, for the sake of individual expression, is Steve Haworth.

~~ STEVE HAWORTH: 3-D BODY ARTIST ~~

The *1999 Guinness Book of World Records* has named Steve Haworth the "Most Successful 3-Dimensional Artist" in the world.* The stunning results of his work are pictured throughout this book. His medium, unlike other artists', is skin. He spe-cializes in implanted jewelry, "laser"-cautery branding, and pseudosurgical refor-mations of the body. His genius lies not only in the subcutaneous implanting of beads, captive rings, and transdermal spikes and jewel casings but also in the cre-ation and manufacture of specialized instruments to effect the work.

"I started working on developing surgical instruments as a child," said Steve. "My father had a manufacturing plant for opthalmalic instruments, and he would bring home cow eyes with cataracts. He would then ask me what kind of instrument we should use to most effectively remove the cataract. If there wasn't anything in the instrument set, I would design a tool." The work of designing a surgical instrument propelled Steve into the business of manufacturing piercing jewelry at a time when the burgeoning field had little such jewelry available. His firm, Haworth Tech Company, still manufactures innovative jewelry.

"People who wear my jewelry under the skin stand out in a crowd" Steve

---

*Steve Haworth operates HTC Body Adornments in Phoenix, Arizona. He has been filmed in over twenty-seven documentaries both domestically and internationally and has been featured in numer-ous magazine articles, newspaper stories, and television shows. He is also an internationally known photographer and his photographs are currently part of a seventeen-country tour.

observes. He has implanted vertebrae-like beadings down the arms of several clients (see pages x, 31, and 73), crosses in the sternums and foreheads of other clients (see page ii), reptilian foreheads, and five generations of horns in Enigma, a former member of the Jim Rose Circus (see page 104). Steve explains Enigma's five implants, saying, "We started with small horns and gradually stretched the skin to accommodate the size that he has now, implanting larger and larger ones over time. It was a slow process, until Enigma got the results he wanted." Always creating cutting-edge designs for implants, Steve's latest work with transdermal implants is pictured as spikes on a shaved head (see page 52). He has added to this work the implanting of jewel casings at the base of the neck, in which precious stones can be interchanged (see page vi).

Steve also does cautery-scalpel branding. "I call it laser-cautery, although it isn't really a laser," he explained. "By using a cautery-scalpel, I can create lines from under one-sixteenth of an inch to those as wide as anyone would want them," he adds. In order for a Caucasian person to keloid properly (to achieve a raised, branded look), that person has to remove the scab on the design as soon as it appears. The repetitive scabbing and healing forces scar tissue to build up and thus creates the raised surface that is the hallmark of branding.

Ear restructuring or reformation is another specialty of Steve's practice that requires an extended knowledge of cartilage and healing. Steve has reshaped ears to resemble a cat, pictured on Katzen (see page 70), and has also made "Star Trek" pointed reformations. "To create a pointed ear," Steve said, "I must first remove the entire lower earlobe. Then the real work begins. I make three tiny incisions, going under the skin to completely separate the cartilage in three strategic areas. I then fold it over, creating a triangle shape, and tape it up with surgical tape." The healing time for this restructuring is about thirty days, at which time the tape is removed and the ear has healed in the desired shape.

As an artist, Steve approaches his creation of 3-dimensional skin art with a particular spiritual devotion. "The first thing I do, when I walk in to do the work, is place a firm hand on the client and look them in the eye. This way I'm really seeing them and they are really seeing me." The purpose of Steve's deliberate touch and eye contact is to create an energetic connection between himself and the initiate. Then, after letting that energy linger for a moment, he begins his own ritual for creating a skin piece. Setting the mood for deep work involves carefully choosing the background sound (he prefers to listen to Dead Can Dance while working), checking that the area in which the work will take place is aseptic, and ritually

**Steve
Haworth.**

placing the instruments while making sure that all the necessary ones are set up for the procedure.

"Then I take a few moments to change my conscious state with some deep breaths while I hold the scalpel. This is when I gather inner peace before making the first cut." Elaborating on the change of consciousness, he added, "When I begin to work I get a sort of 'tunnel vision.' I can only focus on the area that is receiving the modification." The background fades away as he enters into a consciousness that includes only him and the living canvas before him. The stage is set for a powerful initiation to occur in a ritually contained setting, with the conscious tending of the process by the artist and the trust and submission of the client.

The materials for 3-dimenstional skin art are all FDA approved for implantation. Spikes, crosses, transdermal jewel casings, and the specialty pieces he creates are 316L stainless steel and titanium, while the beads and horns are virgin-grade Teflon. At the request of one client, Steve created an ankh with a hollow stem for implanting. The client had lost a loved one and packed the ashes of the deceased in the hollow before Steve sealed the base of the piece. The piece was then implanted in the client's sternum, at the heart chakra. Having the remains of the loved one near his heart, the client experienced joy and sorrowful tears at the outcome of the process.

Besides implanting, Steve has done many penile subincisions and tongue splittings. He remarked, "Although I've done tongue splitting on both sexes, men request this procedure at a ratio of five to one over women." He added, "I think the reasons for tongue splitting vary from shock value to sexual advantages. But there are also some clients who strongly identify with reptiles or dragons and want to replicate the split tongue of the creatures."

One client on whom Steve has worked is Jesse Jarrell, a twenty-one-year-old sculptor who designed and shaped the Teflon riblike pieces that are implanted on the bicep of his left arm (see page 69). Jesse says that the artist Geiger inspired his choice and execution of the design, with the ribs serving as "bionic reinforcement" of the nondominant arm. He chose to have these implants in his left arm because of the energetic and strength discrepancy between the dominant right side of his body and the inferiority of the left side. His motivation for these implants was to create balance, or an energetic symmetry, within his body.

Jesse is considering more modification work, with his end goal being "complete alteration and evolution of the body." This goal stems from his belief in reinforcing human body parts with implantable foreign material to create a sort of living robotic. Jesse's familiarity with the flexible uses of metals and Teflon compliments his work as a sculptor. The gradual introduction of implantable metals and carved Teflon into his body is the creation of a living sculpture.

Clients like Jesse inspire Steve Haworth to use the materials at hand in increasingly creative ways. "My motivation for developing jewelry for implantation and for expanding my practice to include unique modifications comes," Steve said, "from hearing my clients say I have made their dreams come true." Those dreams are recurring visions of matching the physical body to what the inner eyes have seen.

Those who arrive at Steve Haworth's studio for unique modifications are already in the process of individuating. Sharing the experience of having undergone deep processing of life material has led them to seek out these particular fleshworks. Steve's work is never chosen on a whim. His limited availability, location, and cost preclude a decision for an implant or reformation to be done without reflection. Yet even if one overcomes the obstacles to obtain this work and has spent time preparing with inner reflection, there is no guarantee that the transformative healing will take place. To optimize this possibility, one must understand the nature of psychic transformation and healing. For this, we turn to the ancient art of alchemy.

Jesse's
bionic arm
implants.

**Katzen
with
pointed ears.**

5
The Alchemy
of Fleshworks

You are taking a walk with some friends one Friday night in a beach town while on vacation. You're all a little buzzed from the drinks in the last bar. As your group approaches a tattoo studio that does piercings too, you all decide to go in and check it out. After looking over a flash board, you decide to get a scorpion on your left shoulder blade. Another person decides to get her tongue pierced. The studio isn't very busy. The guy behind the counter says it'll take about fifteen minutes until the tattooist is free, and that the piercer is available immediately. The group gathers around the girl as she is prepared to get her tongue pierced. Some are laughing nervously, others are watching a television that is playing in the corner of the room. She has chosen the jewelry and is sitting on an examination table waiting. The piercing is done with little sensation. She walks out smiling after receiving aftercare instructions.

Now the tattooist is ready. The tattooist sticks the flash stencil to your left shoulder and you see the design. It looks good. He then makes a dry pass over the area so you can feel the sensation. No problem, it doesn't hurt. Minutes later the buzzing of the machine stops and you have a blue scorpion, about the size of a half-dollar, on your shoulder. All of your friends are nodding and smiling. You feel really good: endorphins are kicking in. You think how it will look at the beach on your shoulder.

The scenes above are played and replayed many times, in many places, by people of all ages. What is typical in these scenes is that the two people choosing to get tattooed or pierced bring little consciousness to the acts. No psychic transformational moment happened for our subjects. No real threshold crossing occurred. Well, maybe they weren't looking for either. Perhaps this tattoo and this piercing were about adornment. But self-adornment is a continual process that changes as our self-image changes over time. Our two subjects will probably not be happy with the impulsive marking and piercing a few years later.

Even though these scenes are typical, we have already seen that it is possible for body modifications to be much more than a process of self-adornment. By looking now at the ancient art of alchemy we can begin to understand why body modifications have moved into modern life with such force and see the levels of psychic transformation that are possible though these actions.

TORMENT OF THE METALS

Alchemy, reputed to have its roots in either Egypt or China, is the teaching dealing with the transmutation of base metals into gold. The art gave rise to later cryptic drawings and formulas that purported to contain the ancient secret of the transmutation. Today, as we read and attempt to decipher the ancient texts, we note that although alchemy appears to concern itself with the literal making of gold, there is another level on which it can be understood. Alchemy can be viewed as a formula for psychic gold-making, or soul-making. The gold that is made through alchemical processes is other-than-ordinary gold. When we equate it with soul-making, we see that its creation doesn't happen every day under normal daily routine conditions. It is an arduous, difficult, and painstaking operation, requiring patience, determination, and conscious attending.

The stages through which a base metal must pass before becoming this extraordinary gold mirrors the psychological movement of a person becoming who he or she is meant to be: a person in the individuation process. Before we deal with the specific acts of body modification, a brief discussion of alchemical processes and their symbolic colors, as they relate to the human psychic condition, is in order.

**Tattoos,
piercings,
and implants.**

In alchemy, the base metals in need of transmutation are called the *prima materia,* or prime matter. This *prima materia* has to undergo many difficult process-es to render it pure enough to begin the transformation to gold. Those processes will reduce it to an undifferentiated state: a state so malleable and pliable that no rigidity or form exists for it. It is then ready to begin its transmutation to gold. Similarly, in order for you to have the optimal transformative benefit of the body-modification experience, your psychic state should be at a place of pure *prima materia.*

What you had to go through to arrive at that point, what tortures you had to suffer, are the result of six stages of psychic preparation: *solutio, calcinatio, coagu-latio, sublimatio, mortificatio,* and *separatio.** These stages are preparing you for the chance to make psychic gold: the alchemical stage of *coniunctio.* Without having undergone these first six stages, you leave the piercing studio with a lovely piece of jewelry, a wound to heal, and the propensity to either repeat the experience or try another avenue to arrive at psycho-physical satisfaction and satiation.

Solutio means dissolving. This stage returns differentiated matter to its melted and dissolved state; it reduces differentiated matter to *prima materia.* This stage could manifest in you in three ways: you could have dreams in which you are drowning, your house is flooding, it's raining heavily and you are walking in the rain, or you are at the beach and a huge wave washes you out to sea (and varia-tions on those themes); you could have a life experience to which your only response would be to surrender to your fate; or you could have a combination of the two: a watery dream reflecting a challenging life experience.

The point is that your ego position has to dissolve and surrender to something new that it has never experienced before. Because the ego doesn't relinquish authority, even to destiny, without a fight, sometimes during this stage you will feel dismembered and fragmented—without a leg to stand on, without an earthly foothold.

Once your ego has surrendered to its fate, the heat of the situation will cook you. This is the *calcinatio* stage of alchemy. Fire burns all traces of the rigid, fixed ego position to white hot ash. After having dissolved, you are put into the fire and

---

*Following the model put forward by Edward F. Edinger, we will use the Latin terms for these pro-cesses.[26] The English translation of these words refers to the way chemistry defines the principles of matter. In alchemy, the Latin terms encompass not only the chemical processes but also the develop-ment of the soul or spirit.

reduced still further. This is the fiery purgatory of soul-making. Ash has the connotations of mourning, repentance, death, and despair. These feelings are all consistent with a difficult life experience to which you must surrender control. That which is sacrificed in fire is made sacred. Smoke rises. From this reduced ash state ascension may come—although it is not a sure thing. For in alchemical work, no outcome is ever guaranteed. But it may come.

Solutio is associated with water, *calcinatio* with fire, and the next stage—*coagulatio*—with earth. After the fire has burned the *prima materia* and smoke has risen, there remains a residue in the vessel. *Coagulatio* is about finding the pure earth after the heat has driven the impurities out. What this means in psychological terms is that after the dismemberment of dissolving, surrendering, and being tortured by fire, the ego remains intact. Not rigidly fixed as it was before undergoing the other two operations, but still aware of itself and its position.

To use the decision to get a genital or nipple piercing (which offer more extreme sensation than an ear or librette) as an example, a concretization of the first three processes might look like this:

You have been with your partner for many years in a loving relationship. Things are going smoothly when one day, after a routine physical exam, the doctor calls your partner back for more tests. Your partner is diagnosed with a disease that often is fatal. You both share shock and tears: more tears than you have ever shed in your lifetime. Your partner decides to seek treatment. The treatment is long, expensive, and devastating to body and soul. The treatment fails, and you nurse your partner until death.

You will never be the same after having experienced such a loss. Your innocence and naïveté about life and death are lost. Alchemically you have suffered the tears of dissolving in grief, the fires of hopeless and painful treatments, and the earth of remaining in life after one you love has died. This is alchemy in action. Coming out of this experience, you have changed. However, the processes don't stop there.

To conclude a *calcinatio* stage, archetypal contents of the unconscious are brought to consciousness. Nightworld death comes into dayworld life. Coagulation, or the meeting of outer and inner worlds, is the hallmark of *coagulatio.*

Although a portion of the pure earth is left in the vessel (the ego remains intact) after *coagulatio,* that which rises in the smoke (still part of the *prima materia*) undergoes *sublimatio* to further purify the matter. *Sublimatio* is a process concerned with air. "Sublimation does not always denote an ascension, [it is] a process by which substances become more precious, splendid, and excellent—yet it is true that the vapour ascends."[27]

This process resembles distillation in that when the solid matter is heated, it ascends to the top of the vessel, where a cooling takes place. In this cooling, matter resolidifies, this time with the impurities removed. Alchemists view this process as a time where the spirit separates from the body and takes a position of lofty observance. To use our scenario of a loved one dying, with the process of *sublimatio* the survivor suddenly has a view of the grand scheme of life and death that was previously obscured.

If one has a belief in the eternity of the soul or in death bringing about a divine union, this is *sublimatio* imagery. In dreams, flights of birds, magic carpets, climbing staircases, going up in elevators, and flying are all *sublimatio* imagery. What goes up must come down. That is the nature of gravity and of alchemy. So when the lofty, cooled vapor begins to fall back into the bottom of the vessel, it falls hard. This sensation is associated with the blackest and most negative operation in alchemy: *mortificatio.*

Depression, defeat, darkness, torture, mutilation, and death are part of the affect associated with *mortificatio.* Who has not experienced death? The death of a dream, the death of a loved one, the death of a way of life, the death of hope, the death of the past . . . the affect or visceral sense of these moments signals *mortificatio.*

The stench of slowly rotting material composes the complementary process of *putrefactio. Putrefactio* breaks structures down. The acridity and bitterness is removed by the salt of tears, and the resulting material is rendered soft and sweet.

Life is a compost of feelings. We live the scraps of joys and disappointments and relegate them to the rubbish heap of our past. Compost rots, and through that rot emerges new regenerative life. There is always a possibility of rebirth and regeneration through *mortificatio.* The devastated spirit rejoins the body for a resurrection of the soul. This is the capacity of a *mortificatio* process.

With these processes under your belt, are you ready for a truly transformative body-modification experience? It would seem so, but there is one more step in the process. This next step is crucial to making the experience an agent of soul-making, or gold-making. This last stage of alchemical work before the final transmutation is *separatio.*

The ego's fixed and rigid position is now dissolved, burned, distilled, and has been subjected to decay and rot. What remains to happen before transmutation is a final separation of the true essential elements of the psyche from the chaos of the past and the processes under which it has gone. The *prima materia* is almost pure enough for gold-making.

This is the moment when the ego becomes aware of the unconscious and the necessity for sharing power. The ego also becomes aware of itself. This split awareness is a precondition for transformation. "The element *separatio* that ushers in conscious existence is the separation of subject from object, the I from the not-I. . . . To the extent that the opposites remain unconscious and unseparated, one lives in a state of participation mystique, which means that one identifies with one side of a pair of opposites and projects its contrary as an enemy. Space for consciousness to exist appears between the opposites, which means that one becomes conscious as one is able to contain and endure the opposites within."[28]

We have seen this dynamic before in the opposition between the ego and the repressed contents of the unconscious. This dynamic is called naming and integrating one's shadow. This act is not easy to do. If it were, we would all be ready for soul-making, and every body-modification act would yield extraordinary gold.

Returning to the story of loss of a loving partner: You have survived the loss. You attend bereavement group therapy and spend a year in mourning. Slowly you get your affairs in order. You clean out the loved one's closet and give away some clothes. You repaint the house and decide to sell it. You begin to think about dating and socializing. You now spend most of your day thinking about the issues at hand and less and less of it thinking about your loss. You move on with your own life.

This is *separatio* in action. Cutting away from the past, discriminating, discerning differences, and making tough decisions that will change your life are all part of the *separatio* process. Logical thinking, or "logos," is the great agent of *separatio* that brings consciousness and power over nature—both within and without—by its capacity to divide, name, and categorize.[29] Working with the body part that needs healing and understanding why it does, and accessing the energetic needs of the chakras that speak for a fleshwork, are acts of *separatio*. Adequate *separatio* is so crucial to a transformative experience that without it failure is almost predetermined.

The ultimate goal of all the alchemical processes (the *opus magnum:* the great work) is the production of the philosopher's stone—extraordinary gold. This gold is the psychological equivalent of achieving an integration of the ego and the unconscious through an acceptance and acknowledgment of the personal shadow. Gold-making is not a guaranteed feat, nor is it a one-time life experience. The pagan psyche is a complex and multifaceted realm with many sides that begs expression, attention, and healing. So even if one has endured the torture of the psychic metals (psychic preparation), and has, in full consciousness, walked into a studio for a tattoo, piercing, implant, or other body modification, there remains one more alchemical stage for the *prima materia*. This stage will determine whether or not the wounded face that the soul has shown us may be healed. It is only through the final act of *coniunctio* that either other-than-ordinary gold is made or fool's gold is created.

⟫⟫ UNION OF OPPOSITES: *CONIUNCTIO* ⟪⟪

Once the six stages of psychic dismemberment—*solutio, calcinatio, coagulatio, sublimatio, mortificatio,* and *separatio*—are completed one is then prepared to submit to a guide, or adept, for a sensate experience. This is the crowning moment in the tattooing, piercing, implanting, or other body-modification process. In alchemy it is called the *coniunctio.* This is the moment when the metals, purified and reduced to their state as prime matter, undergo the final stage and make other-than-ordinary gold.

Simply put, *coniunctio* is pure consciousness achieved through a union of opposing positions in the psyche. It is from the alchemical stage of *coniunctio* that psychic transformation occurs. But arriving at a point of *coniunctio,* as we have seen, is anything but simple. Shadow projections are a major impediment to achieving full consciousness. Only one who is able to carry one's shadow projections—to hold, simultaneously, the opposites that pull you apart—can experience *coniunctio.*

The *coniunctio* may happen in two different ways: as lesser *coniunctio* or as greater *coniunctio.* It is the greater *coniunctio* that is the desired result of a tattooing, piercing, or other body modification, but more times than not, it is the lesser that is attained.

When a lesser *coniunctio* experience occurs, the subject almost makes the big leap to an integrated consciousness but, for reasons that we will investigate, is

Hand implant and scarification on chest.

destined instead to continually repeat the threshold experience of choice. A lesser *coniunctio* experience might look like this:

You have undergone a trauma. It might have been emotional or sexual abuse, an addiction, a devastating loss, or, more likely, something is out of balance and you can't explain exactly what or why. You decide to get a tattoo of an image that has been plaguing you for some time. You get the tattoo, and the stimulation of the needles leaves you feeling great. Something has shifted as a result of that tattoo. But the effects don't last. A few months later, after the healing is complete, you think about another one. This time another body part needs the marking. Or perhaps the original tattoo doesn't feel finished or large enough. So you go back to the studio for more work. Again, it feels great . . . for a while. . . . Then the urge for some kind of stimulation and healing and scarring comes back, and you decide to get your nipples pierced.

Each time you have made a conscious decision to have the work done. You have chosen the most comfortable studio. You have a bond with your tattooist or piercer. You enter the ritual feeling low and leave feeling high. You have brought some attention and intention to the process but never feel complete for long. Why?

In alchemy, a lesser *coniunctio* occurs when the elements in the vessel have not been properly separated. Psychologically, this translates to one not having identified the source of the trauma before going in for the marking. The marking, implant, or piercing alone will not heal a person of the original trauma that has signaled a body part for work. The ego should have already discerned the unconscious motivations for body modification before entering into the final process. This is the essence of adequate *separatio*.

Fleshworks are most effective when placed on a body part stimulating a particular chakra where memory has consciously located a wound and named that wound. In this way fleshworks bookmark a soul-making event as a sensate threshold is crossed. Fleshworks alone are not designed to produce gold: they function more like shovels in the mine of the psyche, digging for buried gold.

In a lesser *coniunctio*, the tension of the opposites (the unconscious trauma and the ego's ignorance of it) is contained in the person who is seeking a marking. The ego has softened from its rigid position enough to realize that there is a wound in the psyche. The unconscious has opened to the ego to reveal a peek at its shadow elements. The ego, after initial elation of the fleshwork, touches the unconscious briefly and then feels the defeat of that contact because the ego does not understand what it has seen. The fallout of a lesser *coniunctio* is that one may return to a state of *mortifacatio* (depression and defeat) and feelings of further *separatio* (distinction between the act of having gotten the fleshwork and the motivations for having it done) becoming often as uncomfortable as before going into the studio for the first time. Alchemically, the product of this *coniunctio* is maimed, dismembered, and in further need of purification. In the real world, a lesser *coniunctio* is evidenced by one being on a hamster wheel of repetitive tattooing, piercing, or combinations of many body modifications.

The purified union of the ego and the unconscious is what creates a greater *coniunctio. Purified* is the operative word here. This purified position means that one has identified, understood, and assimilated one's shadow. To "own your own stuff" is to stop projecting it out. The philosopher's stone (other-than-ordinary-gold) is a prize that few attain even once. The stone (personified) says of itself, "I am the mediatrix of the elements, making one to agree with another; that which is warm I make cold, and the reverse; that which is dry I make moist, and the reverse; that which is hard I soften, and the reverse. I am the end and my beloved is the beginning, I am the whole work and all the science is hidden in me."[30]

In this marriage of opposites, the ego has to let its rigid position die so that a new perspective may be born. This new perspective embraces the knowledge that opposites (such as good and evil) are a natural and important part of the psychic condition. This concept offers a new sense of self-awareness, greater tolerance, and the freedom to express oneself. It is through *coniunctio* that one evolves further to become who one is meant to be.

BLOOD AS THE PHILOSOPHER'S STONE

As we have said, the goal of the *opus magnum,* or great work of alchemical processes, is the production of other-than-ordinary gold, or what alchemists call the philosopher's stone. How blood relates to this desired end product is that blood, or in alchemical terms *aqua permanens,* is the universal solvent—the liquid form of the philosopher's stone. In psychology, the philosopher's stone is equated with the totality of the integrated psyche.

Blood as the universal solvent is red. In alchemy, colors inform the alchemists of the *prima materia*'s progress in transmutation. As metaphor, alchemical colors indicate the state of the psyche as it attempts to become gold. There are three colors that are primary in alchemy—black, white, and red—each relating to three basic stages of alchemical operations.* Black is the color of the nigredo of matter suffering. We suffer until blackness disappears. Then there is a whitening. White is the albedo of the ash of dawn. This is an ideal and abstract state of mind. It feels good to be in the albedo, full of hope and dreams. Yet dreams vanish if not put into action. So we move to red: the redness of life, the redness of action. Red is the rubedo of blood that reanimates matter to dissolve the last flecks of blackness that may be hiding in the white. When blackness is thoroughly dissolved, one has integrated the shadow (or the devils of the psyche), and a profound unity of body, spirit, and soul is achieved.[32]

What is required for this unification is a baptism in blood. "Baptism in blood, like the encounter with fire, refers psychologically to the ordeal of enduring intense affect. If the ego holds, the ordeal has a refining and consolidating effect."[33] The ego must soften but not break down to endure this intense process. What happens in the decision to modify one's body is a literalization of this psychological baptism. One subjects oneself to intense sensation, corresponding to intense affect. In the moment of a needle or laser piercing the flesh there is a meeting of inner and outer worlds. If one has undergone the alchemical torture of the metals, this matrix is often experienced as a sense of the Divine or an actualization of the numinous.

But why blood sacrifice?** What conditions of this time in history have brought blood ritual into the culture in such a dramatic way? The answer lies in the realm of religion. The mythology of Christianity has lost its hold on the consciousness of the culture. "Our Christian doctrine has lost its grip to an appalling extent, chiefly because people don't understand it any more."[34] Its symbols have lost their meaning. Just as the charge of ancient mythological archetypal religious symbols have waxed and waned for their followers almost to the point to extinction (for example, the ancient Greek gods and goddesses), so goes the Christ symbol. We have discussed its failure to contain light and shadow elements of the psyche, and the necessity, in Christian mythology, for the shadow to be projected out.

....

*This is not to ignore that in ancient texts there was the addition of yellow. Each color corresponded to an excessive humor in the body. White was phlegmatic (excess phlegm); yellow was choleric (excess yellow bile); black was melancholic (excess black bile); red was sanguine (excess blood).[31]

**For a detailed account of the history of blood sacrifice in the ancient world, see Walter Burkert, *Homo Necans: The Anthropology of Ancient Greek Sacrificial Ritual and Myth,* trans. P. Bing (Berkeley: University of California Press, 1983).

If body modifications are the blood sacrifice of the tortured metals of psychic life, if a body-centered self-therapy is holding a key to an individual's attempt to an integrated psyche, then those who choose to engage in these blood rituals are attempting to do what Christ could not. They are attempting to model and contain an integrated psychic life themselves. From this integrated place—through each body that drips blood—an attempt is made to contain the spectrum of good and evil within oneself and to deliver the cosmos from projected evil.

In alchemical language, each man and woman who suffers the tortures of the metals in preparation for such a role earns the name "servator cosmi"—preserver of the cosmos.[35] This is an awesome responsibility. This is a step in a global change of consciousness. The appellation "servator cosmi" will not be given to all who modify their bodies. Yet for all who cross this threshold are these words: we never forget that which has cost us blood.

Librette and ear piercings.

6
The Body as Soulscape

✺ THE URGE TO INDIVIDUATE ✺

As we have seen, the force of patterns of the collective unconscious compels one to become who he or she is meant to be. This adaptation to one's inner truth, regardless of one's conscious truths or purposes, is the urge to individuate. This is not a one-time journey. Individuation is not the end of the road, arrived at on a deathbed. Rather, it is a dynamic process equivalent to the alchemical torture of the metals and the resulting *coniunctio*. Picture a Slinky, a coiled spring. We start at one end of the spring and make the first loop through the individuation process. At the end of each cycle, we arrive some distance from where we began, but ready to make the loop again.

The ego takes an active part in this transformational process, making decisions along the way that cause suffering, conflict, and feelings of dismemberment: all in service of psychic growth. The suffering aspect of the process stems from the conflict generated by the ego's attempt to integrate and reconcile its own ego consciousness with the shadow elements of the psyche. The conflict is necessary for individuation.

In electing to cross a sensate threshold—to obtain some form of body modification—the ego has to relinquish its drive for control of what will happen at that crossing. The conscious decision to cross a sensate threshold opens the ego to the unconscious and, potentially, to all that is contained in that realm. In relinquishing control of knowing what will come and allowing for new and unknown experiences, the ego is striking a bargain with the shadow elements that fear the light of day and would rather remain unknown. Fortunately the ego is secure enough in its position that it trusts it will not be flooded, fractured, or overwhelmed by the contents of the shadow when it becomes aware of them. The continuing process of individuation calls "for a self-acceptance that includes dark aspects of the personality as well as the light conscious ones."[36] At the moment that one decides to get that first tattoo, piercing, implant, or other body modification, the bargain between the ego and the unconscious to accept and integrate the dark aspects of one's personality is struck.

Another way to characterize individuation is to see it as a process of differentiation. As we seek to express the multiple selves that make up our rich and multifaceted psyche, there may be roads that we take to separate ourselves not only from others but from the past in which we have safely operated our lives. Individuation involves taking risks: risks of success and risks of failure. The alchemy of the psyche is shown in the individuation process.

A person choosing to effect a fleshwork has entered the dynamic of the individuation process, even if that process has begun unconsciously. The hallmark of individuation is that those engaging in the process have found an inner dialogue between the ego and the unconscious more compelling than a dialogue between their extroverted persona and others. This inner dialogue may promote the alchemical steps one takes toward a *coniunctio* experience, it may reflect one's immersion in one or more of the alchemical stages, or it may reflect the end result of the alchemical torture of the psyche—the making of psychic gold.

Once in the individuation process, the result may be either a lesser or a greater *coniunctio*. The individuation process, like the *coniunctio* experience, is not a once-in-a-lifetime undertaking or event. There are infinite faces of the soul or psyche that show themselves at various stages of personal development, asking for attention. The inner dialogues change; the psychic issues that require attending change. Individuation is a lifelong process, and regardless of successes or failures one encounters on the journey, all is in service of changing *prima materia* to *ultima materia* and becoming who we are meant to be.

≈ SOUL HISTORIES ON SKIN ≈

The following portraits of people who have crossed thresholds of initiation are slices of real life. When you look at the pictures, you may not think that their piercings are unusual or remarkable. The tattoo images that these people have chosen and the placement of those markings may not resonate with your sense of aesthetics. You may think that tattoo magazines have many more interesting and provocative pictures. All that may well be true.

None of that, however, negates the significance of these body modifications. Our purpose in these portraits is not to compare tatoo and piercing aesthetics. Instead we are listening to personal myths: personal myths with bookmarks. Those bookmarks happen to be imprinted on or punctured in skin. In reading these abbreviated soul histories, in listening to each voice, notice how the markings or piercings emerged as a necessary part of each person's psychic development. Notice how they did or did not effect a life change. Imagine, as you read, how you would tell your story, and notice where your bookmarks fall.

✐ Elizabeth Eowyn Nelson:
Piercing as a Portal to the Underworld

"I had been imagining a nose pierce all summer, going so far as to mention it idly in conversation with a few people—a very few people. I enjoyed the titillation in them and in me when we talked about doing something so out of the ordinary. This is not to say that nose piercing, or any other kind of piercing, is at all extraordinary. This is especially true in San Francisco, where the pierce I wanted is considered tame, almost conventional. But at age forty-two, I am older than many women who choose nose piercing. I am not part of the identifiable groups in which piercing is a means of establishing membership. Furthermore, I spend my days working with executive staff of high technology corporations. I participate in meetings with, and make presentations to, CEOs, VPs, and other fairly staid professionals. These people do not encounter many nose pierces in the average workday."

Elizabeth chose Body Manipulations in San Francisco for her piercing. Walking in, she noticed that it was clean, aesthetically pleasing, and professionally managed. After talking to her piercer, she felt confident that she had chosen a competent studio, because there was a discussion among several of the piercers about her request. She learned that, in her case, this nose pierce was unusual. It was posterior on the nose, very close to the cheek, and parallel to the plane of her cheek. Armed with this new information, she decided to trust the skill of her piercer and to proceed with the piercing that she had been imagining for months.

She was led to a cubicle where the piercing spot was marked on her nose. As the piercer took out a very long needle and curved it slightly for smoother entry and exit, Elizabeth drew in a deep breath. The piercer worked deftly and firmly as the needle punctured the hard cartilage of Elizabeth's nose. Mentally, Elizabeth was prepared for the pain, but her body reacted instinctively. "It hurt like hell," she said, "and it bled, but I managed to stay deeply relaxed and grounded in my body the whole time. My eyes watered badly, but that was about it. I think my piercer was grateful. I can't imagine what it must be like to work with someone who panics."

Walking out of the cubicle, she felt very aware of the pierce. Walking down Sixteenth Street and glancing at herself in shop windows, she saw nothing but the gold ring on the side of her nose. It was as if strangers on the street, glancing at her, were focused on her new jewel. She felt as if she had become her nose pierce, although that would change in time. In the aftermath of the piercing, she realized "that the heightened awareness and identification with the pierce [was] part of the power of the ritual." With such a public and obvious placement of a new piercing, the power was amplified.

Her female friends reacted to the nose piercing with shock, joy, and delight. Her male friends found it erotic. Elizabeth believes that her piercing has caused her male friends to expand their imaginations to see parts of her nature that were previously unknown to them and unimagined.

The day after the piercing, she left for an eight-day silent retreat in the mountains in order to work on a book she was writing. Inspired and charged by the ritual experience of the day before, she said, "I wrote the theoretical chapter of my book manuscript, a pivotal point around which the entire project spun. I placed language that is often used to pin something down in service to imagination that escapes pinning down. I explored what it is like to live in a numinous world, and I titled the chapter 'Living in the Midst of Immensities.' It was an attempt to find the *coniunctio* between Eros and Logos and it required a new level of consciousness to do so. As an opening to the world and the [use of the] word in a new way, I naturally wondered if the new opening in my body—the nose piercing—was instrumental."

Whether this piercing served as a portal for new energy to stimulate the third

**Elizabeth's
nose ring.**

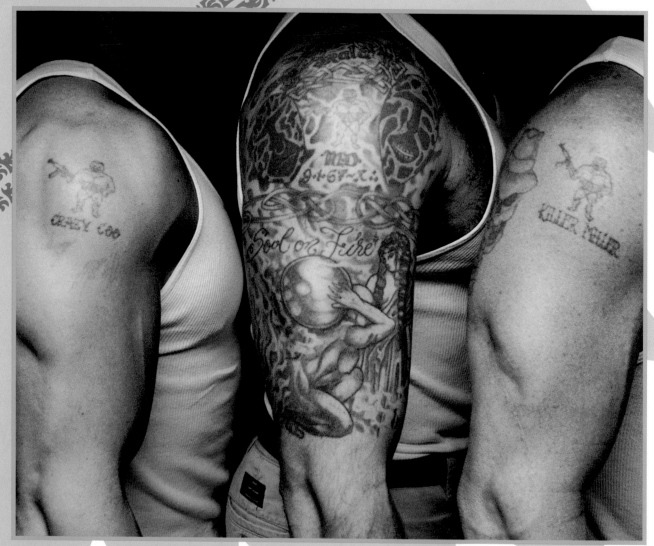

Tattoos of "the Monkey Boys." Left to right: Dave, Mike, & Tim.

eye chakra and promote inner sight, or whether it opened to remove impediments to normal daily sight, dramatic and life-changing events unfolded in the nine months following Elizabeth's nose piercing. She sold her home in San Francisco and followed a waking dream that told her to move south. She finished her Ph.D. course work and found the subject for her doctoral dissertation. She began Jungian analysis and uses active imagination to deepen her creative work, and her sense of home aesthetics has changed from Spartan functionality to soft and comfortable. Finally, she uncovered a deep family secret—that she was given the name of a dead sister—and she changed her birth name to honor both her dead sister and her newfound self.

She stops short of attributing all of these events to the nose piercing. However, she does admit that the power of undergoing a blood ritual, such as this piercing, can penetrate deep levels of the unconscious and open one to one's destiny.

Today, reflecting on her piercing experience, she says, "Piercing can be a portal to the underworld, which is not a place so much as it is what is unknown and unknowingness itself. To quote from the Sumerian poem that describes the descent of the goddess Inanna to this place, 'the ways of the underworld are perfect. They may not be questioned.'"

The Monkey Boys & Tattoo Totems

Tim, Mike, and Dave are listed in federal government indictments as "the Monkey Boys." The name was never one they themselves called their alliance. As Tim tells it, "A group of guys would hang out under a tree at Cleveland High School. They were called 'the Monkey Boys.' Some of those guys did work for us, and we [Tim, Mike, and Dave] got labeled from them. We never used that name." The story of these three guys and their tattoos is one of high drama.

The year was 1987. Dave and Mike were already partners in selling drugs and in "ripping off" drug dealers for their stashes to resell. They augmented their incomes by holding up drug dealers at points of sale and taking their cash. Tim owned a gym where Dave worked out. He then met Mike, and the three of them became fast friends. The threesome were soon driving convertible Ferraris and sporting handguns. They were living fast and well.

As their network grew, Tim, Mike, and Dave stayed tightly aligned. Dave recollects, "We didn't have a gang. There were just a loosely organized group of people working for us holding up dealers and selling drugs." The three had a pact:

everything that came in got split three ways. There was no exception to that rule. In a world where no one could be trusted, they trusted each other exclusively. Mike said, "This was our code of honor."

As a testament to that trust and pact they decided to get tattooed. In 1988 there were few shops or artists for tattooing. They found one, a jaded Vietnam vet who could do the work. The image they chose was a bodybuilder holding a gun: each man got his nickname put under the image. Tim's tattoo had the name "Killer Miller"; Mike's tattoo was MED, which stood for "the doctor"; and Dave's tattoo said "Crazy Coo," a nickname he had gotten in high school.

According to Tim, the bodybuilder with guns had real significance to them. He said, "Our main weapon on the streets was the intimidation factor. People understood that if you crossed one of us, you had to deal with all three." The three were all buff, well built, and big. The bodybuilder tattoo reflected their physical strength, the guns their intimidation, and the names their individuality. After the tattooing, they saw themselves as the Three Musketeers. Sharing the tattooing experience together and sharing the image solidified the three men in their commitment to honor their code of "all for one and one for all."

This tight alliance had many informants approaching them to help set up drug dealers. Mike said, "The informants would be given a cut, but the bulk of the take was always divided three ways. No matter how big the tip or how big the score, nobody got in with the three of us."

This time of easy money and drugs could not last. Federal government agents and local law enforcement were slowly building cases against the three. In 1990, Tim was sent to prison for "extortion and coercion." He was the first to go, serving two and one-half years. When he got out, his share of the cut, accumulated while he was away, was waiting for him.

During the time that Tim was away, Mike was sentenced for "assault with a deadly weapon" and served three months. Then Dave, who had avoided all of the other charges the Feds had tried to level against him, was convicted of counterfeiting. He was caught in a sting operation in 1993 and served six years in prison. Tim, who was then out on parole, was also caught with the counterfeit bills and sentenced for that. Back in prison, he served another two and one-half years.

An update to the history finds the three wanting to remove the tattoos of their alliance. This is not surprising, because although the markings were important to the three at the time they got them, for each of them that period of their lives is one that ended badly. Prison sentences separated them, their cooperative enterprises crumbled at their separation, and with time, they outgrew the risk-taking behaviors of their youth. Tim is doing stunt work for movie and television studios. Dave is in the security business, selling alarms and home protection devices, and Mike runs a small supermarket chain. By law, they are not allowed to associate with each other. Their tattoos, which once spoke of their unity, have lost their meaning and their charge. The tattoos marked a time in their lives that will never be repeated: a moment of their personal histories, imprinted on skin.

✍ Kathleen Loughery: The Power of Marking

Kathleen Loughery of InnerSight is a practicing psychic intuitive and shamanic counselor, currently living in the Hawaiian Islands. At the time of her decision to get a tattoo, she was living in the Limahule Valley on Kaui. This valley is considered, by the Hawaiians, to be a sacred place where ancestral spirits roam amidst medicinal plants and lush foliage.

A series of synchronicities led her to the design of her tattoo, the colors of the image, and her understanding of the power of the ritual of getting tattooed. The first event was the meeting of her soul mate Chris. Chris was extensively tattooed with Hawaiian tribal images. When Kathleen expressed interest in getting a marking herself, he drew her a complex Celtic image that mirrored exactly what she had envisioned and was sized correctly for her placement. Of the design, Kathleen said, "He had no idea of my Celtic connection, or my connection with a Celtic cross." Although she resonated with the design, she sought extra guidance through a tarot card reading. She said, "I kept choosing the High Priestess . . . and over and over again when I asked about the tattoo, I kept hearing, 'High Priestess marking, High Priestess marking.'" The cards assured her that the design was correct.

The drawing was without color. After choosing a local tattoo artist, Kathleen dropped off the drawing for coloring suggestions before making the actual appointment for the tattooing. When she returned the next day, she had already made up her mind that the tatoo would have blue, green, purple, and orange tones. "When I got there," Kathleen said, "she handed me the image, colored in exactly the colors I had in mind. I knew it was a sign. So I made an appointment for the next day."

When she is working with clients, Kathleen's psychic readings and counselings are delivered while she is in a self-induced trance state channeling spirit guides. The trance state causes a split in the psyche, and Kathleen is dissociated (or split-

Kathleen of
InnerSight.

off) from her body for short periods of time. In her case, this bodily dissociation is not new. Kathleen began dissociating from her body at a young age as a result of sexual abuse. Kathleen chose to place her tattoo on her lower back near the base of the spine. This turned out to be a healing placement for Kathleen because the energies around sexuality, reproduction, fertility and creativity, and generation of new life located at the base of the spine (the base chakra) needed release from their blockages.

The day of the appointment, Kathleen had some anxiety about the sensation she would experience getting the tattoo. She recalls that day: "To deal with the sensations of tattooing, I took a ritual bath at home and spent some time looking in the mirror and doing affirmations. When I got to the tattoo parlor, I knew I would be picking up everybody's energy around me. So I immediately created a wall of energy around me and held a large crystal. When I sat down and she started working, at first the pain actually grounded me—brought me fully into my body. But then the pain also began to trigger my body memories of sexual abuse. It triggered the incest. I don't know why it actually did."

Kathleen, overwhelmed by physical pain and psychic pain, acted instinctively, slipping into a semidissociated trance state. She began to chant, and holding the crystal she directed the pain up her spine, through her body to the crystal, and out her hands.

Speaking of the pain of tattooing, Kathleen remembers, "I established an energy flow first and then the visions started. The sensation opened up almost every single physical abuse pain I had ever experienced: which was rape, invasion, being beaten . . . all kinds of images. What would normally happen, when the psyche starts to reveal those kinds of images, is that my body would spasm. It would either experience a physical flashback, or it would experience something in order to stop it . . . stop the flow of it.

"What the tattoo experience did was allow my body to stay intact with the memory. The merging of those forces produced an enormous healing in me. I realized I couldn't leave my body and that the visions were not going to stop. It was like a video library of visual images that came through me. As the vision of the painful experience came through me, I was physically feeling the pain in the area of the tattoo." The vision and the physical pain were related because the abuse had happened in the same chakra. Kathleen was holding the visions, the body memory of abuse, and the present physical pain of tattooing all simultaneously. What emerged for her was a healing chant, "This is my pain and I own it. This is my scar.

I own what has happened to me. I own my scarring. This is a way for me to scar myself. No longer will these things be embedded in me."

After a time, she recalls, the sensations shifted. "Vision after vision, energetically in the body . . . coming through . . . coming back out. I felt nothing. I felt no pain. I felt a gentle energy that came from the needles. I felt that what the needles did was merge something in my psyche. They merged my physical life experience with my psyche, which had had a hard time with the fragments of the painful memories.

"What happened to me after the tattoo is that my entire life shifted, because my perspective shifted. It was as if through this opening that was created in this tattoo, the energy that was held and lodged in my body came through in visions, in pictures . . . and came out. That is the only way I can describe it. As a result, I started losing weight and I allowed myself to have an intensified sexual experience that led my body to respond in a sexual way it never had before. It was as if someone went in and Roto-Rootered it right out. That's what happened. At thirty-four years old I was able to fully heal . . . fully heal. Now, it has taken years and a lot of different practices to get to this point, but it was the tattoo that healed the part of me that needed to come through, which was the sexual part. As a result, I've matured. I've become not the little girl, I've become a woman. And to me the tattoo is not just a marker, it was through the experience of it that this happened. It changed my life."

⁓ Oren Cohen: A Living Canvas

Oren Cohen is an artist as well as a singer and bass player with his band Zeroephect in Los Angeles. His body is a rich landscape of his life experience reflected by numerous tattoos and piercings. Oren believes that each tattoo and piercing marks the healing of a psychic wound, or a grid point on the map of his spiritual journey. Although there may be other avenues for healing, Oren chooses tattoo images and piercings because of the combination of the charge of the images and the sensate threshold he must cross to actualize these images.

He began his personal canvas when he was sixteen. The first two tattoo images he drew himself. A large open-centered sun with irregular blue and green flames encircles his left nipple, with a large, black tribal gecko under the nipple, curving around it in the empty center of the sun.

"The sun," said Oren, "is actually a water symbol, because the flames are ocean

**Oren
Cohen.**

colored and moving like the ocean. The lizard is an earth sign for me. I've always envisioned the earth's surface like the scales of a lizard." He says he chose the breast area "to ground" him and keep him centered. "It's right over my heart," he added.

The tattooing was done in two sessions. Oren did not know the artist beforehand, but the shop was chosen because they did not ask for identification to verify his age, and it was very clean. The first session lasted three hours and the second, four. "The first session was the most excruciating pain I had ever felt. He outlined the entire design first, which was a deeper needle, and the gecko's foot is on my nipple," he reported, "So that was really bad." Afterward he felt "totally flushed and exhausted."

The second session took place five days later. "That was surprisingly easy," he said. "My body adjusted to it and I felt I had control over the pain." He said he felt that the pain was gratifying. "It felt good to hurt so bad. Thousands of little wounds get to be healed. It makes you feel all the much better when they heal."

Oren was proud at having endured the pain. He noted, of the tattooing process, "Whenever you inflict pain on yourself it forces you to heal yourself, and pulls you deeper inside yourself than you could normally be. Pain is very therapeutic and very necessary to feel anything at all. It is very humbling."

There are several aspects to Oren's first tattooing experience that can be amplified. His personal situation and state of mind at the time he chose to get his first marking directly influenced his design, color choice, and tattoo placement. His home life was fractured by his parent's divorce, and his decision to live one week with one parent and the next with the other parent was psychically dismembering. He survived the exhausting weekly adaptations to changing environments by dissociating from his body, which had been thrust into an emotionally painful situation. Thus it is not surprising that, his situation being "up in the air," he would choose to actualize the three elements that were missing for him: earth (the gecko), water (the blue and green colors), and fire (the sun image). Although he had a sense that his heart chakra needed healing and that these elements were necessary, he was not entirely conscious of how his decision to tattoo his breast would effect a healing. The initiation of pain provided him with a rite of passage across a significant threshold. He said, "If I could endure this tattooing, I can endure anything."

Almost a year later he got another tattoo. This time it was on his right, inner forearm. The image is his name in Hebrew characters. He deliberately placed it on the same spot Holocaust victims were tattooed with their prisoner numbers. He chose this tattoo not only in an attempt to name himself but as an acknowledgment to those who had died for his right to exist. He felt that if they had to be marked, he had to be as well. "There's no reason for people not to know who I am and what I am," he said. He also added that he was very disappointed that this tattoo was not painful to receive.

Again, Oren was in a painful life situation at the time of this tattooing. He had quit high school and moved, alone, to a new city to enter a trade school. The youngest student at the school and living alone in a strange city, he felt anonymous. The tattooing of his name gave him an identification with his roots. His desire for the tattooing to be painful may be seen as his desire to actualize the pain of his loneliness through his body. His disappointment is a sign that this was a lesser *coniunctio* experience for him.

In the last four years Oren has added to his body art. His left foot is jeweled and banded with a tribal turtle motif wrapping around his Achilles tendon. Working as a chef at the time of this tattooing, he said he felt the urge to tattoo his foot, "to stabilize his situation and ground the experience of working hard for someone else." It is important to note that this job was not a creative outlet for his cooking talents, nor was this a productive time in his life artistically. So the left foot tattooing, although useful for Oren's reasons, was also an attempt to stimulate the artistic, creative energies that were being repressed.

A traditional fifties-style hula girl was added at the base of Oren's spine, as was a female figure that Oren calls "Madam Pele," the Hawaiian fire goddess, tattooed on his left arm. He feels that Madam Pele is "of the underworld and powerful." He added, "The underworld is where all of our roots and anchors are. She's lava. She's fire. She's the powerful forces of nature. My reason for getting her is that you need one strong woman in your life. If I can't find one on this plane, the image speaks for that need and provides psychic armor [from the pain of that lack]."

After the healing of this image, Oren got his nipples and navel pierced. He explained this choice saying, "I needed these piercings to serve as a wake-up call for me. Like when somebody has a heart attack and they get a jolt to revive them, I got the thickest and most painful nipple piercing I could. A couple of people turned me down for these piercings, because they didn't want to put me into jewelry that thick. I did it and I nearly passed out when I actually got pierced. But it definitely did what it was supposed to do. I was in a horrible place in my life, working eighty-plus hours a week doing something I didn't want to do, around people I hated, in a place I hated. Creatively and psychically I was dead. I needed to jump-start myself and kick the part of me that was in a coma in the ass. I did. These piercings started me on a journey out of my hole. I had no illusions about it. I did it because I wanted it to hurt, and it hurt bad. I wanted to have the long healing process of it—it takes a year to heal these. As a side thing, aesthetically, I love them. But that wasn't my initial drive for doing it. I wanted to feel the pain and I wanted to have the scars on me as a testimony to that pain," he explained.

Following the piercings, a lotus flower tattooed at the base of his neck balanced his spine (with the hula girl at the base). He then tattooed his right bicep with an armband of peony flowers, which hold special significance for him. "These have always resonated with me," Oren said. "They're the only things that will give themselves to you and be most beautiful just before they die. They are white in life and assume color in death. They only harvest once a year and their fragrance is amazing. You can literally watch them be born, mature, and die."

He is currently completing a dragon emerging from the flames surrounding Madam Pele on his left arm. This tattoo is very complex and although the outline of the entire dragon curves down his arm and on to his hand, he is in no hurry to complete the coloration. "This piece," he says, "is a work in progress. It mirrors my life at the moment. I just want to complete it slowly and enjoy the process."

✐ Rebecca Joanne Buelow: The Cat

Rebecca Joanne Buelow is a twenty-one-year-old model who has tattoos, piercings, and implants on her body. She appeared on her first magazine cover in December of 1998 with *Tattoo Magazine* and has appeared on three more skin-art-type magazines covers since, in addition to being in many other photographs that are now in print.

She began her body modification work when she was sixteen with a tongue piercing because a friend dared her to do it. Within the two years that followed that piercing, Beki got a second tongue piercing, her nipples pierced, an eyebrow piercing, a navel piercing, and a nose piercing. After the initial tongue piercing, she developed a trusting rapport with her piercer, and got her subsequent piercings exclusively from him.

After turning eighteen, she changed piercers. This time she chose a woman in a different shop. It was with her that Beki got a librette* piercing. In Beki's words,

---

* A librette piercing is located between the bottom lip and the chin. Beki had a traditional barbell inserted so that the tip of the silver ball is visible on the face. It is also possible to insert a ring that encircles the bottom lip.

Rebecca with implanted captive bead rings.

"It was this piercing that was my rite of passage piercing. It was directly on my face, and I had a job that didn't like piercings and was giving me an ultimatum of not working or not having the piercing. I think this is when everything started to change for me. I quit my job because I wasn't going to live unhappy. And my librette piercing has made me very happy."

Her librette piercing, she felt, was the beginning of the public face that was uniquely hers. It was the first obviously conspicuous piercing, with the exception of the delicate eyebrow piercing, and it could not be concealed. Shortly after this piercing, she developed a master plan for the tattoo work that would become her signature look.

The master plan for her tattoo work incubated a long time before she was conscious of exactly how it would be executed. As a child, her grandmother was very influential in her life. With her parents having divorced when she was five, she was shuttled back and forth between changing households for most of her life. Her grandmother was a constant fixture in a changing world. This matriarch gave pet names to each of her grandchildren. Beki's was "the Mouse." Beki said it reflected her childish squeals of joy and also her grandmother's perception of her that she had a passive and yielding nature. These perceptions were deeply held, and Beki rebelled against them.

She saw "the mouse" change into "the cat." Beki entered a tattoo studio in Phoenix and began talking to an artist named JJ about her plan to become "the cat." Almost immediately after the conversation, he started a series of spots on her upper back that spilled over her shoulders, around her breasts, and down the top part of her arms. After three hours of work, he stopped, and Beki scheduled her lower back and hips to be completed in another session. This tattooing began Beki's transformation from "the mouse" of her childhood. She explained, "I move, act, and have features like a cat. I'm grown up now. I can act the cat. I can take over a dominating role in my life as the cat."

The tattooing on her body is extensive. She admitted that "ever since [getting those tattoos], it's become a massive addiction for me. I mean smelling green soap, hearing tattoo machines . . . ; it puts me in a total trance. You know, actually feeling the tattoo machine burning across my skin is an experience all of its own."

Her relationship to Steve Haworth introduced her to the world of implants. After they became romantically involved, they decided to concretize their commitment by Steve giving Beki captive bead ring implants. Beki chose her inner forearms for these rings. The placement, she felt, was feminine, nonobvious, and powerful in that her forearms were the strongest parts of her arms. She had been assisting Steve with his implanting work for many months, and now she assisted in preparing for her own. "I set up the implant itself . . . got everything out and ready to go. It was about a half-hour and a bucket of tears later that they were in, with no problems, in the center of each of my forearms. I cried . . . I cried so much through the whole thing. Not because of the pain, and not because of its being so odd. It was just an incredible step in our relationship and it brought us so much closer to each other than anything ever could . . . any card . . . any ring . . . any flower, anything could have done."

Beki's implant work didn't stop with the captive bead rings. She has recently gotten a transdermal placement in the center of her chest. This implant, anchored under the skin, has a small threaded exposed hole in which custom jewels may be inserted. The effect is as if a jewel is floating on the skin, where a necklace pendant would normally sit. Beki explains why this implant has importance beyond its decorative function, saying, "My breastbone has a dent in it. The bone structure is malformed and threatens to grow in and damage my heart. I don't want the bone to be broken and reset, even though doctors have said it is a surgery that should be performed."

Beki has chosen the transdermal jewel casing as the fleshwork of healing for this wound. This is the path of healing she has followed all her life. She acknowledges the artists who have helped her color and sculpt her physical body to match her inner vision of herself, saying, "I'm grateful for everything I have ever received from my tattoo artists and my body-modification artists. I love them. They have helped me to become the way I'm supposed to be. My body modifications are reflections of my soul."

There is never one reason why an individual chooses to engage in body modification. Regardless of what tattoo image one chooses, what piercing brings one pain or pleasure, or where an implant is placed, the motivations behind the choices are multilayered. Factors such as present life situations, childhood dreams and disappointments, past traumas and triumphs, and a host of imaginary forces that stir the soul all contribute to the flavor of the fleshwork.

The sketches we have seen are single voices in a choir of many. Each has chosen to hear the soul's voice by engaging in an inner dialogue. Each has used his or her body as a vehicle of attempted healing and transformation. This inner dialogue of personal soul is a precursor to a greater dialogue: a dialogue with the soul of the world.

**Enigma
with fifth
generation
horns.**

7
The Landscape Expands

With the increase in the speed of communication, with the advances in global information sharing, there has been a corresponding decrease in Western man's feelings of relationality and connectedness to place, ancestors, and roots. As an interesting historical and social parallel to the seventeenth century that we explored in chapter 2, we see again today a decrease in man's feelings of potency and personal significance in the wake of our ever expanding knowledge of uncharted territories of the cosmos. In addition, at this time in history, there is another deconstruction that has jangled our psychic nerves: the dominant religion of the West, Christianity, is in its demise.

Communities and social groups of people are united by their shared faith in the tenets, laws, and rituals of their mythology. In times past, the powerful archetypal symbols of Christ, the Virgin Mary, and Satan carried the projections of good and evil for the majority of the Western world. What has happened to this two-thousand-year-old mythology is that its archetypal symbols have lost their charge and meaning for many Westerners.

This did not happen overnight. There has been a gradual decline in the relevance of these symbols to the experiences of Western people in daily life because of Christian mythology's failure to provide archetypal symbols that model an integration of good and bad, light and shadow.

Personal numinous images that appear in dreams, waking visions, and altered states of consciousness have no place in traditional religious hierarchical structures. Traditional monotheistic religions do not reflect the rich spectrum of a pagan psyche. The archetypal actualizations of a polytheistic psyche, so necessary for personal growth and individuation, break ancient molds. Owing to this situation, "when the archetypes have no adequate container such as an established religious structure, they have to go somewhere else because archetypes are facts of psychic life."[37] So what happens when God and Satan get fired from their jobs? Where does that leave us?

⸎ THE BODY ENSOULED ⸎

There are four possible responses to the loss of religious archetypal structures: (1) with the loss of the god-projection through the church, the individual will lose his or her connection to the Self; (2) an individual will assume the projected qualities of the fallen deity and succumb to inflation and hubris; (3) the withdrawn projections will be reprojected onto a secular or political movement [as was the case with Communism]; or (4) with the projections thrown back onto the individual, back onto the self, he or she may discover the god-image within his or her own psyche.[38] In other words, we are left cooking alchemically in our own vessels.

In addition to the lack of religious archetypal support, the rational, logical, and biological ways we have of functioning in the modern world also do not address our need to resolve the irrational wholeness of life.[39] Old ways of projecting shadow, or evil, on people different from ourselves no longer make sense as racial and cultural barriers are breaking down. We are left feeling that "once the traditional symbol system breaks down, it is as if a great surge of energy were returned to the individual psyche, and much greater interest and attention then becomes focused on the subjectivity of the individual."[40] This extreme focus on and interest in the subjective experience of the individual has never before received the level of attention and importance that it has today.

Some of us choose this inner scrutiny consciously: some engage the inner-self unconsciously. Those who engage in the ritual fleshworks of tattooing, piercing, branding, implanting, and other body modifications are concretizing and literalizing archetypal drives for personal growth. By using the body as a vehicle for self-discovery, individuals are driven to explore the limits and parameters of sensate response: the exploration mirroring the drive for transpersonal experience.

As we have said many times before, even if one undergoes all of the alchemical operations in a vessel of his own making, there is no guarantee either that a transformation of consciousness will actualize or that the fleshwork will bring about much-needed psychic healing. But the implications of the attempt at a conscious healing of body and soul cannot be ignored.

By engaging in this extreme inner scrutiny, either through a dualization or in the contemplation of a fleshwork, a bridge between ego consciousness and deep levels of the unconscious is formed. This bridge functions as a mediating conduit between the ego and inner voices and, by extension, between integrated whole consciousness and the world.

Imagine the possibilities for understanding differences among people if we accept the multiple voices within ourselves and listen to what they say. Imagine the increased capacity for negotiated settlements of disputes in families, communities, nations, and the world if we understood the nature of shadow projection and were consciously working on containing and integrating our own shadow elements. Imagine what schools and jobs would look like if spontaneous images of the collective unconscious were encouraged and nurtured: if activities of daily life were seen as valuable rituals and were honored, if we took the time to write and discuss our dreams.

The body is the human landscape of world soul. Its boundaries of flesh and ego are artificial and unable to be defended against the soul of nature that is asking to be remembered and asking to be heard. To hear the soul of the world begins with hearing one's own psyche's voice as spoken through the body. This cannot happen without a true sense of what interactions with the world may be conducted through the body.

It is an instinctual drive to search for meaning in one's life through one's exchange with the world. The experiencing body is not a hermetically sealed vessel. We dialogue with the outside world through our senses. Seeing, hearing, tasting, smelling, touching, and feeling viscerally provide open pathways for exploring beyond the body and conversely are pathways for receiving the world into the body. Our senses mediate our experience of the outer world.

A body-centered engagement with the unconscious realms of the psyche, through fleshworks, directly involves the larger world. What if, as through the looking glass, we do not dream, but we are the dream of nature? What if the forces of nature direct the cultural trends that we see around us? Can you invert your thinking to include the possibility that all of our actions are directed by nature, not by our narrow egos?

It is challenging to think that the decision to get a tattoo, piercing, branding, implant, or other body modification is not a decision that we make, but rather it is a move directed by a larger ecosystem screaming for attention. "Nature is always dreaming, unfolding herself in each moment. We, also, dream—each day imagining ourselves into our own inner nature. In the meeting place between natures, a window opens, and we are deeply touched. We remember, for a time, our psychic inheritance, an endowment rooted most essentially in the rhythms of nature."[41]

This is radical eco-psychology. Nature dreams the species on, not the reverse. Initiated and marked individuals are players in the drama of deep ecology.* Deep ecology is hearing into the soul of nature as it is animated and speaking not only to us but through us. Initiated and marked individuals engage deep ecology in their animation and actualization of their soul's voice through the body, and by extension open to the depths of a larger unconscious ground of being: the soul of nature. "The breathing, sensing body draws its sustenance and its very substance from the soils, plants, and elements that surround it; it continually contributes itself, in turn, to the air, to the composting earth, to the nourishment of insects and oak trees and squirrels, ceaselessly spreading out of itself as well as breathing the world into itself, so that it is very difficult to discern, at any moment, precisely where this living body begins and where it ends."[42] Thus, we are the world and the world is us.

By honoring images of the collective unconscious one is opening to a new way of hearing and seeing what in the world unconscious needs expression. This opening expands the ego beyond its boundaries. Knowing the world's needs begins with a recognition of what the individual body needs. If the body is crying for attention and healing, is it not reflective of a louder world voice?

---

*The term *deep ecology* was first coined in 1973 by Arne Ness, Professor Emeritus of Philosophy at Oslo University in Norway.

Tattooed arm and librette piercing.

ANIMA MUNDI: THE SOUL OF THE WORLD

We relate with deep intimacy to the world. The matrix of our interaction bespeaks the soul of each thing, the soul of all matter touching the soul of our personal matter. Whether natural or man-made, aesthetically pleasing or hideously ugly, we meet in connection; we confront each other face to face. It is difficult to think that a building has soul, a computer is soulful, an old stuffed toy contains a soul spark. Yet dispute that the building that appears in your dream does not have something to say, does not claim your attention. Consider what your dream car, the car you wish you could afford, says to you and about you. Think about "a healthy business," "a lean bank account," "lively music." We do not animate these images. They stand, autonomously animated, on their own. "An object bears witness to the image it offers, and its depth lies in the complexities of this image."[43]

Just as tattoo images don't stand for anything (they stand on their own), the images of the world present in their particularity. Lizard presents itself as lizard. A split tongue presents as it is. The clock on the desk has its own form. They exist with their own depth and complexity, just as we do. When we begin to see the world as having value and meaning through our witnessing of it, not our use of it, and not our subjective interpretation of its meaning, we can begin to hear the voice of it.

The obvious benefit of this deep appreciating and listening is a reconnection to the Divine Soul through the world. We recapture a way of being in the world that is almost extinct, if not alien to Western thought. What we are relearning to see are the gods and goddesses reflected, not only in all people, but in all there is. A pagan vision of the world.

This form of attention and witnessing of the world deepens our capacity for understanding what feeds and nourishes our own souls. A decision to tattoo, pierce, brand, implant, or modify the body in some other way will be accompanied by noticing and giving attention to what the body wants: what the body is saying. That the body speaks is a reflection of the world speaking. Here is another alchemical process: the mutual feeding of world soul to individual soul called *cibatio*. The fire and life of one feed the fire and life of the other. In this mutual feeding, both are served, both are nourished.

To change an old system of thought or behavior requires nothing short of a revolution. There is a revolution occurring today. It is subtle and very slow moving. Many do not see the large wave of movement of the underbelly of this revolution.

They look at increased violence among people, markings and brandings of their children, and divided families and do not see the tsunami approaching behind the waves. The world is speaking through our every movement. Individuals who understand the nature of consciousness through acceptance of the unconscious are pushing that wave to shore.

Whether working consciously through the sensate body with a fleshwork or contemplating life situations from an alchemical perspective, these people are expanding human consciousness. This is the new paradigm for the next century: the world speaks through us and we speak through the world. When conscious-ness expands to take in this relationship, one cannot help but be changed. It is by changing ourselves that we effect greater change around us. The soul of the world is heard.

Everyone has a particular version of the creation of the world. Each version is its own myth, resonant to the one retelling it. We offer this work as an opportuni-ty for those who read it to find their own personal myth. When you review your life, when you tell a slice of life story, you have animated the archetypal moments in a long and complicated tale. Heroes and demons show up. Struggles and tri-umphs abound. Through initiatory rites you bookmark a soul scar in time and move to another level of personal growth.

Alchemical symbols and processes chronicle soul scars. Tattoos, piercings, brandings, implants, and reformations mark those places where psychic gold gets made. We have offered you a means of ritualizing the archetypal motifs, moments, images, and numinosum of your life experience in the creation of your own myth. Indeed, "the defining feature of myth . . . is its connection with ritual."[44] Through that ritualizing comes an honoring of our connection to all sacred in life, and to the soul of the world.

Notes

1. James Hillman, "Psychology—Monotheistic or Polytheistic: Twenty-five Years Later," *Spring* 60 (1996): 122.
2. Ibid., 113.
3. James Hillman, *Re-visioning Psychology* (New York: HarperPerenial, 1976), 137.
4. Rufus C. Camphausen, *Return of the Tribal* (Rochester, Vt.: Park Street Press, 1997), 29.
5. Edward C. Whitmont, *The Symbolic Quest* (Princeton: Princeton University Press, 1969), 163.
6. Ibid., 105.
7. Richard Tarnas, *The Passion of the Western Mind* (New York: Ballantine Books, 1991), 278.
8. J. Bernstein, "The Decline of Rites of Passage in Our Culture: The Impact on Masculine Individuation," in *Betwixt and Between: Patterns of Masculine and Feminine Initiation,* ed. S. Foster, M. Little, and L. Mahdi (La Salle, Ill.: Open Court Publishing, 1987), 138.
9. Arnold van Gennep, *The Rites of Passage* (Chicago: University of Chicago Press, 1960).
10. Michael Harner, *The Way of the Shaman* (New York: HarperSanFrancisco, 1980), 20. Michael Harner, Ph.D., is the founder and director of the Foundation for Shamanic Studies, Norwalk, Connecticut.
11. Ibid.
12. Maureen Mercury, "Transformation through Ritual" workshop for the Association of Professional Piercers, Las Vegas, Nevada, May 26, 1998.
13. Harner, *The Way of the Shaman*, 50–51.
14. Victoria Lautman, *The New Tattoo* (New York: Abbeyville Press, 1994), 9.
15. Ibid.

16. Michelle Delio, *Tattoo: The Exotic Art of Skin Decoration* (London: Carlton Books, 1995), 65.

17. Camphausen, *Return of the Tribal*, 115.

18. Victoria Lautman, *The New Tattoo*, 14.

19. Thanks for this part of active imagination to Dr. Stephen Aizenstat, Pacifica Graduate Institute.

20. James Hillman, *Healing Fiction* (Woodstock, Conn.: Spring Publications, 1983).

21. Neil R. Carlson, *Foundations of Physiological Psychology,* 4th ed. (Boston: Allyn and Bacon, 1999), 4.

22. Leo Zuleta, Black Wave Tattoo Studio, Los Angeles, California, conversation with author, May 1999.

23. Gahdi Elias, Mastodon Body Piercing, San Diego, California, conversation with author, May 1999.

24. James Hillman, "Puer's Wounds and Ulysses' Scar," *Dromenon* 3 (1981): 12–27.

25. Ibid., 23.

26. Edward F. Edinger, *Anatomy of the Psyche* (La Salle, Ill.: Open Court Publishing, 1985).

27. Martinus Rulandis, *A Lexicon of Alchemy* (1612; reprint, Kila, Mont.: Kessinger Publishing, 1992).

28. Edinger, *Anatomy of the Psyche*, 187.

29. Edinger, *Anatomy of the Psyche*, 191.

30. Marie-Louise von Franz, ed., *Aurora Consurgens,* trans. R. F. C. Hull and A. S. B. Glover (New York: Bollingen Foundation, 1966), 143.

31. Edinger, *The Mysterium Lectures* (Toronto: Inner City Books, 1995), 190.

32. Edinger, *Anatomy of the Psyche*, 147. This analysis is based loosely on Jung's 1952 lecture.

33. Edinger, *Anatomy of the Psyche*, 38.

34. "Crazy Times," letter from C. G. Jung to Ruth Topping (November 12, 1959), *New York Times,* 19 November 1993, Op-Ed.

35. Marie-Louise von Franz, *Archetypal Dimensions of the Psyche* (Boston: Shambhala Publications, 1997), 50.

36. Edward C. Whitmont, *The Symbolic Quest: Basic Concepts of Analytical Psychology* (Princeton: Princeton University Press, 1969), 177.

37. Edward F. Edinger, *Ego and Archetype* (Boston: Shambhala, 1992), 64.

38. Ibid., 67–68.

39. "Crazy Times," letter from C. G. Jung to Ruth Topping.

40. Edinger, *Ego and Archetype*, 69.

41. Stephen F. Aizenstat, "Nature Dreaming: Depth Psychology and Ecology," unpublished article, 1994.

42. David Abram, *The Spell of the Sensuous* (New York: Vintage Books, 1997), 46–47.

43. James Hillman, *A Blue Fire: Selected Writings by James Hillman* (New York: HarperPerenial, 1989), 100.

44. Walter Burkert, *Homo Necans: The Anthropology of Ancient Greek Sacrificial Ritual and Myth,* trans. P. Bing (Berkeley: University of California Press, 1983), 31.

Bibliography

Abram, David. *The Spell of the Sensuous.* New York: Vintage Books, 1997.

Aizenstat, Stephen F. "Nature Dreaming: Depth Psychology and Ecology." Unpublished article, 1994.

Bernstein, J. "The Decline of Rites of Passage in Our Culture: The Impact on Masculine Individuation." In *Betwixt and Between: Patterns of Masculine and Feminine Initiation,* edited by S. Foster, M. Little, and L. Mahdi. La Salle, Ill.: Open Court Publishing, 1987.

Burkert, Walter. *Homo Necans: The Anthropology of Ancient Greek Sacrificial Ritual and Myth.* Trans. P. Bing. Berkeley: University of California Press, 1983.

Camphausen, Rufus C. *Return of the Tribal: A Celebration of Body Adornment.* Rochester, Vt.: Park Street Press, 1997.

Carlson, Neil R. *Foundations of Physiological Psychology,* 4th Edition. Boston: Allyn and Bacon, 1999.

Delio, Michelle. *Tattoo: The Exotic Art of Skin Decoration.* London: Carlton Books Ltd., 1995.

Edinger, Edward F. *Anatomy of the Psyche: Alchemical Symbolism in Psychotherapy.* La Salle, Ill.: Open Court Publishing, 1985.

——. *Ego and Archetype.* Boston: Shambhala Publications, 1992.

——. *The Mysterium Lectures.* Toronto: Inner City Books, 1995.

——. *The Mystery of the Coniunctio: Alchemical Image of Individuation.* Toronto: Inner City Books, 1994.

Eliade, Mircea. *Rites and Symbols of Initiation: The Mysteries of Birth and Rebirth.* Dallas: Spring Publications, 1958.

Harner, Michael. *The Way of the Shaman.* New York: HarperSanFrancisco, 1980.

Hillman, James. *A Blue Fire: Selected Writings by James Hillman.* New York: HarperPerenial, 1989.

———. *Healing Fiction.* Woodstock, Conn.: Spring Publications, 1983.

———. *The Myth of Analysis.* New York: HarperPerenial, 1972.

———. "Psychology—Monotheistic or Polytheistic: Twenty-five years later." *Spring* 60 (1996): 111–125.

———. "Puer's Wounds and Ulysses' Scar." *Dromenon* 3 (1981): 12–27.

———. *Re-visioning Psychology.* New York: HarperPerenial, 1976.

Johnson, Robert A. *Inner Work: Using Dreams and Active Imagination for Personal Growth.* New York: HarperCollins, 1986.

Jung, C. G. *Alchemical Studies.* Trans. R. F. C. Hull. Princeton: Princeton University Press, 1983.

———. *Psychology and Alchemy.* Trans. R. F. C. Hull. Princeton: Princeton University Press, 1993.

Lautman, Victoria. *The New Tattoo.* New York: Abbeyville Press, 1994.

Mercury, Maureen. "Transformation through Ritual." Unpublished article, 1998.

Rulandis, Martinus. *A Lexicon of Alchemy.* 1612. Reprint, Kila, Mont.: Kessinger Publishing, 1992

Tarnas, Richard. *The Passion of the Western Mind: Understanding the Ideas That Have Shaped Our World View.* New York: Ballantine Books, 1991.

van Gennep, Arnold. *The Rites of Passage: A Classic Study of Cultural Celebrations.* Trans. M. Vizedom and G. Caffee. Chicago: University of Chicago Press, 1960.

von Franz, Marie-Louise. *Archetypal Dimensions of the Psyche.* Boston: Shambhala Publications, 1997.

———, ed. *Aurora Consurgens.* Trans. R. F. C. Hull and A. S. B. Glover. New York: Bollingen Foundation, 1966.

———. *Projection and Re-collection in Jungian Psychology: Reflections of the Soul.* Trans. William H. Kennedy. La Salle, Ill.: Open Court Publishing, 1980.

Whitmont, Edward C. *The Symbolic Quest: Basic Concepts of Analytical Psychology.* Princeton: Princeton University Press, 1969.

Acknowledgments

This book was created as is a mosaic. At the center of the grand design was Oren and his tattoo journey, and spiraling from that, Pacifica Graduate Institute, Barbara Keiller, Cliff Bostock, Jane McGoldrick, Jon Graham at Inner Traditions, Steve Haworth and Beki Buelow, Jeaneen Lund, the beautiful tattooed, pierced, reformed, and modified people who wanted their souls to be understood, Chris Ward the computer wizard, and Jeanie Levitan of Inner Traditions, without whom, the final picture would not have been completed. May this book be a herm for their journeys.